Taking
Care of the
People
who Matter
Most.

A Guide to Employee-Customer Care

Sybil F. Stershic

Taking Care of the People Who Matter Most.
A Guide to Employee-Customer Care

ISBN-10: 1-934229-04-0
ISBN-13:978-1-934229-04-0

Editor: Yvonne DiVita
Cover Design: Maslow Lumia Bartorillo
Page Layout/Design: Karin Marlett Choi

Published by:
    WME Books
    Windsor Media Enterprises, LLC
    Rochester, New York
    USA

Available online at: **www.WMEBooks.com**, as well as
other booksellers and distributors worldwide.

Special Sales:
This and other WME Books titles are available at special
discounts for bulk purchases, for use in sales promotions,
or as premiums. Special editions, including personalized
covers, excerpts of existing books, and corporate
imprints, can be created in large quantities for special
needs or projects.

For more information, please contact:
    Special Book Orders
    Windsor Media Enterprises, LLC
    282 Ballad Avenue
    Rochester, NY 14626
    1-877-947-BOOK (2665)
    info@wmebooks.com

Dedication

To Michael and Jason with all my love.

Acknowledgments

I didn't know it at the time, but the seeds of this book were planted when I started my career more than 30 years ago and found myself applying my educational background in social psychology to my first marketing job. It's been a true labor of love to finally get it in print and to quell my husband's echoes of "Write the book already!"

There have been so many wonderful people along the way who have helped me reach this point, and I thank them all. Among them I want to acknowledge some very special colleagues, clients and friends (in no particular order): Peg Portz, Frank Haas, Chris Bonney, Mike McDermott, Toby Bloomberg, Debra Semans, John Bartorillo, Phyllis Barr, Bob Wood, Mike Bartoszek, Linda Diehl, Susan Danoff, and Linda McAleer.

I would also like to extend my gratitude to Leonard L. Berry and Stephen W. Brown for serving as my mentors in services marketing and leadership. In addition to Len and Steve, I've been inspired by the work of Christian Grönroos, Don E. Schultz, and Jagdish N. Sheth.

While writing a book is a solitary endeavor, getting it to market is a team effort. My publisher and author advisor, Yvonne DiVita, went above and beyond the call of duty in helping me publish this book. I appreciate her taking on the role of surrogate counselor during some difficult times, many unrelated to the book itself. Special thanks to the editing, production, and marketing staff at Windsor Media Enterprises for helping me make this book a reality.

I also want to acknowledge my friends at Maslow Lumia Bartorillo for the quality creative work they provide for my "brand," including this book's cover design: John Bartorillo, AJ Zambetti, Michael Scholl Heather Colleran, and Shannon Lesniak. Thanks, also, to my personal team of proofreaders: Enid F. Gossin and Charlotte Ravaioli.

As this book is all about taking care of the people who matter most, I need to acknowledge the most important people in my life for their unconditional love and support: my mother and lifelong teacher, Ruth Fischman; my sister, Enid F. Gossin; and my brother, Joel Fischman. I wish my beloved father, David Fischman, and my beloved brother, Bruce Fischman, were here to see this book come to fruition.

And finally, there is my husband and soulmate, Michael, and our incredible son, Jason, who matter more than anything. Thank you for your love, sense of humor, and for making the journey worthwhile.

Table Of Contents

Why I Wrote *Taking Care of the People Who Matter Most: A Guide to Employee - Customer Care*

This is a book about the "care and feeding" of the people who are ultimately responsible for an organization's success. It's about internal marketing — a blended approach focused on taking care of employees so they can take care of customers. It is about marketing, and human resources, and management, and creating a positive customer-focused culture.

I have studied and practiced internal marketing throughout my 30+ year marketing career: collecting and sharing examples of best practices, writing about it, and presenting it in workshops and conferences across the United States. In the past few years, however, I've seen increased interest in the concept of internal marketing as managers are eager for new and proven ways to better engage employees for strategic advantage. These managers have come to recognize employees — the people who embody and deliver on the brand promise — as the organization's true differentiators in today's highly commoditized world.

Management and human resource books abound on how to compete for the best talent in a tight labor market where companies have to work harder to attract and retain employees. But employees shouldn't be treated with any less attention when the unemployment picture changes. Addressing the economy's transition from low to high unemployment in 2003, a *Fast Company* article acknowledged: "In many workplaces, the message has changed from 'What can we do to keep you happy and keep you here?' to 'You're lucky to have a job, so sit down and shut up.'"[1]

The reality is that even in times of high unemployment, managers still need to be concerned with employees' satisfaction and retention. We know that unemployment goes hand-in-hand with reduced consumer spending; i.e., when fewer people are working, they tend to spend less. As a result, companies have to work harder to compete for customers. And to effectively attract and retain customers, you need a trained and motivated staff.

What Are the Benefits of a Satisfied Workforce?

Research shows that employees who have better relationships with their companies are more likely to:

- Stay with the company, thereby reducing the high cost of turnover.

- Recommend the company to other potential employees, also reducing search expense.

- Be more productive in their jobs, augmenting the organization's return on its investment.

- Provide higher service levels, increasing customer satisfaction and loyalty.[2]

Apparently, many managers aren't aware of or don't care about reaping the benefits of a satisfied workforce. A recent Maritz® Poll found only 10% of workers strongly agreed that their companies genuinely listened to and cared about their employees[3] (I hate to imagine what it's like for the other 90%!) Look around — how many people do you know who work in organizations that really care about them? And how many are employed in what they consider a toxic workplace?

Taking Care of the People Who Matter Most: A Guide to Employee-Customer Care is more than just a "feel good" book for taking care of employees. Given the complexity of dealing with rising customer expectations and greater workplace demands, managers are challenged with the need to continually motivate employees to sustain high levels of customer satisfaction. Consider, also, the ramifications at the opposite extreme — the negative impact that dissatisfied employees and customers have on an organization's sales, operating costs, morale, and brand image. Given that dynamic, who can afford to ignore the potent power of the employee-customer connection?

This book gives managers the foundation and tools needed to leverage this critical connection. You'll learn a practical framework and applicable strategy for internal marketing that will enable you to be most effective as you communicate with, educate, and motivate your employees to take care of your customers.

Best of all, you don't have to be in marketing to use this approach! Any manager, regardless of functional responsibility, can apply internal marketing tools and activities. After reading this book's examples of how different-sized companies in a variety of industries use internal marketing for employee-customer care, you'll find internal marketing is practical and easily adaptable to almost all organizations in the corporate, nonprofit, and public sectors.

Note to nonprofit managers: the concept of employee-customer care also applies in the nonprofit world. If you are uncomfortable with the term "customer," substitute the appropriate term(s) to describe those constituencies who are important to you: clients, members, stakeholders, donors, or volunteers. In addition, where applicable, consider mission fulfillment in place of references made to corporate bottom-line results.

How to Use This Guide
To Employee-Customer Care

Besides demonstrating the value of the employee-customer connection, this practical Guide provides a solid framework managers can use to develop an effective internal marketing action plan. It starts with a "Mini-Audit" you can use to assess your organization. You'll also learn the foundation of internal marketing strategy along with a variety of applied internal marketing tools to strengthen your employee-customer link and internal service culture.

To help you make the transition from concept to application, several chapters contain "Action Plan Starter Notes" with questions designed to help you apply the insights and ideas to your situation. The Guide concludes with an easy-to-follow Checklist and special Worksheets that will enable you to develop a customized internal marketing action plan for your department/division/business unit or organization.

So read on and learn how you can effectively take care of the people who matter most.

CHAPTER 1

Employee Engagement and the Bottom Line

Dispirited, unmotivated, underappreciated workers cannot compete in a highly competitive world.

Francis Hesselbein[1]

Not long ago, when corporate America was undergoing continuous restructuring, many employees reported feeling unmotivated, unrecognized, and unrewarded. In today's uncertain economy, the situation hasn't changed much. Thanks to business headlines featuring ongoing layoffs and the fallout from corporate scandals, employee commitment is in jeopardy. As a result, management's best efforts to serve customers can be inadvertently undermined by employees who can't rally the requisite energy and enthusiasm needed to be customer-focused.

Why does this matter? It's a simple principle: the way your employees feel is the way your customers will feel. And if your employees don't feel valued, neither will your customers.

As a business professional and consumer, I've seen how employees impact customers. What employees experience in their organizations carries over to customer attitudes and intentions; i.e., employees influence what customers think about your business and determine whether (or not) they'll establish and maintain relationships with your company. Managers who try to cater exclusively to customers while ignoring their employees' well-being in the process are doomed to fail. Smart managers know they need to pay as much attention to their employees as they do to their customers.

In his extensive research on customer loyalty, Frederick F. Reichheld found a direct connection between an organization's treatment of its employees and its customers' resulting attitude toward the organization. According to Reichheld, none of the companies in his research "achieved extremely high customer loyalty without fostering similarly high loyalty among [their] employees."[2] Maritz®, a research firm specializing in customer experience and loyalty, reports that the connection between the employee experience and the customer experience is receiving increasing "attention as a true driver of business success."[3]

Despite this connection, "companies too often ignore the dynamic people issues that are at the core of their customers' experience."[4] Employees are considered an afterthought, even in firms that buy into being customer-focused. Why is this happening when we know employees play a critical role in maintaining and enhancing customer relationships, serving as company advocates, and delivering on the brand promise?

In reality, many executives may openly acknowledge employees as their greatest asset, but operationally and culturally they don't treat them as the company's greatest asset. The most they do is offer them lip service. The authors of a recent book on successful corporate cultures, *Firms of Endearment*, sum it up best: "Like customers, employees have long been objectified — seen as resources for exploitation in service of company objectives."[5]

In a Forum® Corporation study from the spring of 1996 that asked why consumers switched companies, nearly 70% of the reasons given were not product related. Consumers said they switched companies because they felt either the attention they got from the company they left was poor or they hardly got any attention at all.[6] As Jay Conrad Levinson, father of an aggressive grassroots marketing approach known as "guerrilla marketing," acknowledged: "The majority of business lost is lost due to customers being ignored."[7]

So it doesn't matter how much you're spending on the latest and greatest technology, how innovative your products and services are, or how persuasive you are at getting customers in the door. If your employees don't take care of them, they won't be staying long.

I can tell you that public perception of your company's brand is influenced by what you promise in your marketing communications as well as what you (i.e., your employees) actually deliver. As customers interact with your organization, if their experiences are inconsistent or conflict with your marketing messages, what are they most likely to believe: your marketing or their experience?

This is the reason that employees are truly "the most powerful medium for conveying the brand to customers."[8] It's why I advocate an employees-first approach, based on the advice of J.W. Marriott: "Take care of your employees and they'll take care of your customers."[9]

Yet, whenever I share Marriott's philosophy while addressing senior executives, I get the same reaction. I can read it on the faces of the conference attendees whose eyes glaze over as they say to themselves, "Here it comes, the old 'warm and fuzzy stuff.'"

Wrong! Instead of "warm and fuzzy," the evidence is "crystal clear" that customer relations mirror employee relations. Research shows a direct link between employee satisfaction and customer satisfaction, and between customer satisfaction and improved financial performance.[10] As you read on, you'll find numerous other studies cited throughout this book that show the impact that employee and customer satisfaction have on profitability and the bottom line.

Effective employee-customer care is based on the self-reinforcing relationship between employee satisfaction and customer satisfaction. Pay insufficient attention to maintaining the satisfaction of either group and you risk distortion of your organization's brand image and bottom line. To see the true reflection of employee-customer satisfaction, look within your organization.

The View from the Inside Out

Taking Care of the People Who Matter Most: A Guide to Employee-Customer Care is based on an often overlooked, underutilized strategy to create a corporate culture committed to both customers and employees — a strategy of internal marketing. This approach applies marketing inside the organization: to engage employees and instill customer-focused values for organizational success. Its primary focus is on taking care of employees so they can take care of customers.

Consider the evidence supporting the relationship between employee and customer satisfaction. In the 1980s, a bank holding company in Florida commissioned two independent studies: one was a branch customer satisfaction survey, and the other was an employee opinion survey. Researchers found significant agreement among both customers and employees — those branches that ranked high on customer satisfaction were also rated favorably by employees on a number of organizational factors such as management support, empowerment to meet customer needs, internal customer service, training, motivation and the overall quality of work-life.[11]

In the mid-to-late 1990s, Harvard Business School researchers James L. Heskett, W. Earl Sasser, Jr. and Leonard A. Schlesinger demonstrated the progressive bottom-line link between employee and customer satisfaction, employee and customer loyalty, and (ultimately) customer loyalty and profitability. Following are several examples from their book, *The Service Profit Chain: How Leading Companies Link Profit and Growth to Loyalty*, that describe the relationships between employee and customer satisfaction:

- Restaurant chain Chick-fil-A® found 78% of its restaurants with above-average customer satisfaction scores also reported above-average employee satisfaction.

- The operating divisions of Waste Management® with the highest customer satisfaction scores also ranked highest on employee satisfaction and were more profitable than those divisions with the lowest employee and customer satisfaction scores.

- When comparing employee turnover rates, Taco Bell® found 20% of their stores with the lowest turnover had double the sales and 55% higher profits than the 20% of stores with the highest employee turnover.[12]

More recently, the 2006 Maritz® Customer Experience Study found 43% of all customers who defect do so because of customer service issues. The study also found 77% of the time those customers blamed employee attitude as the primary reason leading to their defection.[13]

Let's take a closer look at the internal ramifications of employee satisfaction. How do employees feel about the goods and services their companies provide? Research shows that highly satisfied employees purchase their companies' products and services at much greater rates than employees who are not "highly satisfied." A retail study found 95% of highly satisfied employees routinely shopped at the store where they worked compared with 0% of the dissatisfied employees. The highly satisfied employees were also more willing to recommend their companies' products and services to customers, which can lead to greater sales.[14]

In addition, employees can influence the sale of the organization itself to potential employees. "Unconsciously, your employees enhance or destroy your organization's 'magnetism' or ability to attract new hires every day. . ."[15]

8

And recruitment isn't the only area affected; workplace satisfaction also impacts employee loyalty and retention.

One study on employee loyalty asked employees to assess the likelihood they would accept a job offer from another employer at comparable pay. More than 90% of "highly satisfied" employees said they would definitely remain in their current jobs — that is, they would decline the offer — compared with only 30% of "satisfied" employees, who would also remain in their current positions and decline the offer. Employees at lower levels of satisfaction said they would basically take any job offer they received to get out of their current positions.[16]

Managers would do well to remember that unhappy customers are not the only ones who can choose to leave an organization. Just like the cost of customer "churn," the cost of employee turnover can be damaging, especially when you examine both direct and hidden costs. Direct costs include employment advertising, recruiter fees, increased unemployment tax, and reference checks in addition to the extra time required by human resources and the requesting managers to schedule, interview, and train new hires. Related hidden costs include "loss of organization knowledge, disrupted departments, missed deadlines, low morale, loss of client relationships and chain-reaction turnover."[17]

Numerous human resources research and consulting organizations have estimated turnover costs ranging from 150% to 200% of annual pay.[19] For example, according to one estimate, it costs $78,000 to replace an employee in a $46,000 per year job, or approximately 170% of annual pay. (For a comprehensive guide on how to calculate the true costs of turnover see Nancy S. Alrichs's book, *Competing for Talent*.) When it comes to the bottom line, employee satisfaction, loyalty and retention have as much impact (positive or negative) as customer satisfaction, loyalty, and retention.

Employee-Customer Care: A Blended Management Approach

While it is easy to acknowledge employees' impact on customers, ensuring that impact is a positive one can be a challenge. Throughout my career, I've heard from managers and other executives who understand the employee-customer connection but are unsure how to best influence it. They all want to know: how do you get employees to work with you rather than against you?

The answer can be found in internal marketing, which "enables employees to keep the promises that have been made to customers."[20] Internal marketing involves the application of marketing inside an organization to instill customer-focused values for organizational success. Just as professional marketers use marketing to attract, motivate, and retain customers, managers can use internal marketing to attract, motivate, and retain employees.

Don't be intimidated by the "marketing" label here, since you don't have to be a marketer to apply internal marketing. A comprehensive approach that blends marketing and human resources, internal marketing is best defined as "the ongoing process whereby an organization aligns, motivates and empowers employees at all levels to consistently deliver a positive customer experience that helps achieve business objectives."[20]

While marketing is traditionally thought of as being externally focused — with most of its activities directed at reaching outside markets and customers — the reality is that no organization will be successful without the support of its most valuable internal resource: its satisfied, dedicated employees. Applying marketing internally allows an organization to focus on those representing its true competitive advantage. Think about it: most products and services can easily become commoditized, but competitors cannot duplicate the relationship an organization's employees have with its customers. "Really making your people your most important asset turns out to be difficult for your competitors to copy."[21]

Despite the marketing label, internal marketing is more a management strategy than a pure marketing function. One of internal marketing's early advocates, Christian Grönroos, identified two separate but integrated components of internal marketing: attitude management and communications management. Attitude management involves motivating employees to buy into the organization's customer-oriented values, while communications management involves providing and managing the information that employees need to perform effectively.[22]

11

It's important to understand, however, that internal marketing is not an attempt to create "Stepford" employees — plastic, smiling automatons going about their business, happily serving customers. Internal marketing is an approach that advocates employees be considered upfront, and not as an afterthought, in planning and implementing corporate strategy.

Internal marketing encompasses a range of management and supervisory activities including (but not limited to) training, recognition, empowerment, management support, information sharing, reinforcement and team building. It collectively builds on these and any communications, educational, and motivational efforts used to reinforce the value of customers and the employees who serve them. As such, it is not a totally new concept.

What is distinctive about internal marketing is its proactive, strategic approach focused on both employee and customer care.

How Much Internal Marketing Do You Need?

Despite the evidence linking employee and customer satisfaction, few managers consciously apply internal marketing. In some organizations, management appears cool to the concept, while others are quick to dismiss it as "warm and fuzzy," as noted in my experiences at the start of this chapter.

Why don't these folks implement this great strategy that will improve their businesses? Unfortunately, for most companies, the answer is either top management doesn't see the need for it or thinks the company is already doing it. Such thinking is reflected in these typical scenarios:

- Management's professed concern for its employees is mere lip service. According to the "Dilbert Principle," the statement "Our employees are our greatest asset" tops the list of "Great Lies of Management."[23]

- The organization suffers from "cultural schizophrenia" and purports to be employee- and customer-focused when it's really operations-driven.

- Management assumes everything is OK, so internal marketing is not needed (i.e.,"We have an employee-of-the-month award program and an annual employee picnic . . . what more do they want?")

To see how your organization stacks up, complete the following internal marketing mini-audit. Circle the number that best applies to each statement, and be as candid as possible. (For best results, I recommend you conduct and review this audit with others in your organization ranging from front-line staff to executive management. This will provide you with different perspectives on the need for internal marketing within your organization.)

Internal Marketing Mini-Audit

We're there and feel good about what we are doing	We're working on it and trying to improve	We're clueless; what's the big deal?
5 4	3 2	1

Based on the scale outlined above, to what extent:

Do employees know what is expected of them in helping your organization achieve its goals?

5	4	3	2	1

Do employees really know and understand your customers?

5	4	3	2	1

Are employees given the tools they need to perform effectively (information, training, equipment, etc.)?

5	4	3	2	1

Does management proactively reinforce the importance of customers?

5	4	3	2	1

Do all employees (not just those with direct contact) understand their impact on customers?

5	4	3	2	1

Internal Marketing Mini-Audit

We're there and feel good about what we are doing	We're working on it and trying to improve	We're clueless; what's the big deal?
5 4	3 2	1

Based on the scale outlined above, to what extent:

Is customer information shared throughout your organization (customer wants, needs, expectations, perceptions)?

5	4	3	2	1

Are employees involved in improving customer satisfaction?

5	4	3	2	1

Are employees' efforts to take care of customers recognized?

5	4	3	2	1

Does your organization recognize "internal" customers (i.e., employees)?

5	4	3	2	1

Does communication flow openly throughout your organization (top-down, bottom-up, laterally)?

5	4	3	2	1

15

Scoring the Internal Marketing Mini-Audit

If you circled mostly 4's and 5's, keep up the good work! You are fortunate to be in an organization where management recognizes the value of its people. To help you maintain momentum, use this book for reinforcement and look for new ideas to build on your current efforts.*

If you circled mostly 3's and 4's, you are on the right track. Figure out what you need to do to improve (to get you closer to the 5's) and get others involved throughout your organization to help. Stimulate your thinking with the ideas in this book and network with other managers (both inside and outside your field) to build an inventory of internal marketing tools you can use.*

If you circled mostly 1's and 2's, you have your work cut out for you. Determine what you need to do to move up a notch to 3 or 4. Also, consider who needs to get involved? Who needs to be convinced? Use this book as a starting point for ideas and practical examples of how to be more attentive to your employees.*

Equally important, don't despair if you don't have the authority to effect a change throughout your organization. Instead, concentrate your efforts on a micro level – you can apply internal marketing within your own department, division or business unit.

*You can find additional ideas for internal marketing on my blog found online at: **www.qualityservicemarketing.blogs.com.** My blog is continually updated with content that supports the advice in this book.

16

What if your company continues to resist internal marketing? Then consider other options. The good news is you can find other organizations whose culture and values go beyond lip service to recognize and reinforce the importance of employees as well as customers.

Hiring the right staff and training them to serve customers effectively is a manager's initial hurdle. Once you have the right people in place, the ongoing challenge is how do you continually motivate employees to sustain customer satisfaction? We'll explore the answer to this question in the next few chapters.

CHAPTER 2

Gaining Employee Commitment: A Formula for Success

 "Millions of dollars spent on heavy advertising are wasted if employees do not know, and are not equipped to deliver, the promises that have been communicated to customers."

Ben Machtiger[1]

T he foundation of an effective internal marketing strategy is based on gaining employee commitment. Why does your business need commitment from its employees? According to Lawrence A. Crosby and Sheree L. Johnson of Synovate Loyalty, "Employee commitment results in ... the employees' identification with and attachment to the company, their internalization of its goals, and their willingness to put forth discretionary effort to help it succeed."[2] This discretionary effort is "the extra level of performance people give when they want to do something;" i.e., it's the "difference between commitment (doing it because we want to) and compliance (doing it because we have to ... or else!)."

To gain employee commitment, you need to apply the *"3 Rs Formula"*:

Respect = giving employees the tools they need to do their jobs
Recognition = catching employees doing something right
Reinforcement = continually supporting a customer-focused culture

= *3 Rs for Employee Commitment*

I developed this formula to help managers better understand what's behind internal marketing. Let's explore each of the 3 Rs in more detail.

Respect: Giving Employees the Tools They Need to Do Their Jobs

A company **Respects** its employees when it gives them the proper tools and information they need to do their jobs. **Respect** involves three key elements: communication, training, and empowerment.

Communication

Tell employees what your organization stands for, what its goals and objectives are, and what your organization expects of its employees. This helps employees understand what the company is trying to achieve and how, as employees, they can effectively contribute to the end result. Giving your employees this information — i.e., what their roles are in the "big picture" — may be critical to your company's success, as it's "only when employees understand how they fit into the bigger picture ... that they apply the discretionary effort necessary for the organization overall to excel."[3]

Communication must be open so that employees have access to the information and knowledge they need to perform their jobs. They need answers to basic questions such as:

1. Where is the organization headed and why?

2. What are the implications for the organization's future?

3. What do we employees need to know/do to help us get there?

Specific examples of information organizations should share with their employees include the following:

- future plans, goals and direction

- rationale behind important decisions and actions

- market and competitive impacts

- customer feedback

- product/service performance and new product or service development

- operating policies and performance standards

- benefits and promotion opportunities.

While sharing this type of basic information with employees seems like a no-brainer, many companies fall short in their efforts to communicate this vital content to employees. In a study conducted by the International Association of Business Communicators (IABC) Research Foundation and Right Management Consultants®, nearly half (48%) of the companies studied "failed to effectively explain to employees the purpose of their jobs and the mission and strategy of their businesses."[4] How can employees help your company move forward if they don't know where your company is going or what your company expects of them?

We've known about the impact of organizational communications on employee performance for a long time. As a result of research he conducted in the 1960s, Chris Argyris found that a lack of openness in communications led to reduced employee commitment to organizational goals.[5] Jan Carlzon, former president of Scandinavian Airlines Systems (SAS)™, understood this and made it part of his personal leadership philosophy: "An individual without information cannot take responsibility; an individual who is given information cannot help but take responsibility."[6]

We will learn more about the impact of internal communication on employee performance, when we explore how to strengthen an organization's internal service culture in Chapter 4.

Training

Besides knowing what's happening in an organization, employees also need to develop or enhance the skills necessary to their jobs. Multiple types of training are required:

- operational training
- orientation to the industry
- product knowledge training
- communications and customer relations skills
- management or supervisory training

24

Each type of training expands your employees' knowledge base and strengthens their connection to your organization.

Operational training. This initial training covers the organizational basics that explain an employee's fit and function within the company — how the firm operates; who the key players are; who the customers are; what the organization's mission, structure, and resources are; what the employee's assigned department or division norms are; etc.

These organizational basics are usually shared in the initial stage of an employee-employer relationship, for example, in new employee orientation. In smaller firms that don't have a formal orientation program, new employees obtain this information from their managers and/or co-workers.

Orientation to the industry. While most organizations educate their employees about the company itself, few go beyond the initial orientation to educate employees about their industry. Who are your competitors and how are they performing? Who presents the greatest threat? What trends and market forces are likely to impact the industry?

Industry-related information is available in trade and business publications and is usually found in the executive suite. But why not make these resources available to all employees? If you can't afford to increase your subscription budget, set up a central library or resource area and let your employees know about it. Highlight important industry news or relevant articles and post them on the company intranet.

Similarly, you can request that all staff who attend industry or professional conferences share the information and ideas learned at the conferences throughout the organization. Build in opportunities to continually educate employees about your industry, not only in orientation, but also in staff meetings, brown-bag lunches, seminars and related training events. The better informed your employees are, the better they can perform, including being alert to outside influences and innovative ideas.

Product knowledge training. All employees, even those with limited or no customer contact, should be thoroughly familiar with the products and services your company provides. Who are the appropriate target markets for your products? How can customers maximize product use? How do your products stack up to the competition? Why would a customer choose your product? Why should a customer choose your product? From my own experience as a consumer, I'm continually amazed by the encounters I have with employees who are clueless about their company's products and services.

Communications and customer relations skills. Some of these interpersonal skills can't be taken for granted. Do your employees know how to effectively deal with customers? Do they know how to effectively communicate with other employees, suppliers, or partners? From the fundamentals on how to meet and greet customers to the challenge of dealing with difficult customers, this type of support training can help employees interact more effectively with others.

26

Management or supervisory training. Helping employees develop to their full potential is part of any manager's job description, but not all managers come with the requisite skills or experience to do this — especially new managers. Management development training programs range from team-building to collaboration to assessing employee performance. Unfortunately, because these programs are considered "soft" training, many companies cut back on management development during lean times and do not always reinstitute this type of training when their financial picture improves.

Investment in employee training can yield significant returns. A University of Pennsylvania study of 3000 companies found that 10% of revenue spent on capital improvements boosted productivity by 3.9%, whereas a similar investment in developing human capital increased productivity by 8.5%.[7]

It's important to understand investment in training is not a one-time event. The dynamic marketplace we live in spurs technological innovation in the form of new and improved products and services, resulting in more competition and increasing consumer demands. As the market changes and as companies adapt and evolve, we need to continually upgrade our employees' knowledge and skills.

Empowerment

After *Communication* and *Training*, the final element of **Respect** is Empowerment. Employees need to have a

27

sense of ownership in providing customer care, including serving other employees as "internal" customers. Empowerment involves giving staff the latitude to properly serve customers without asking permission every step of the way to handle basic customer requests or problems. Nothing is more frustrating to a customer than to hear "Sorry, I can't help you" because the employee doesn't have the tools and/or skills to properly take care of the customer.

Interestingly, empowerment can be an important source of employee satisfaction. One company study found about two-thirds of its employee satisfaction levels were affected by just three factors:

1. the latitude given employees to meet customer needs

2. the authority given employees to serve customers

3. employees' possession of the knowledge   and skills needed to serve customers.[8]

Effective communication, training, and empowerment form the cornerstone of **Respect**. In my workshops, I suggest the following mnemonic as an easy way to remember these three elements — explain, train, and refrain:

- **Explain** to employees what their jobs involve and how they fit in the "big picture."

- **Train** them to do their jobs.

- **Refrain** from getting in their way.

28

Recognition: Catching Employees Doing Something Right

Recognition is the second R in the 3 Rs Formula of gaining employee commitment. Whenever possible, you want to catch your people doing something right.

Recognition can be informal or formal, but it need not cost much. What I'm talking about is simple, sincere acknowledgment of an employee who goes the "extra step" for a customer or fellow coworker. Studies have shown the incentives that are most motivating to employees tend to be relatively easy and cost the least.[9] In fact, in a study of potential workplace motivators conducted by Dr. Gerald Graham, professor of management at Wichita State University, employees ranked the following three "no-cost" incentives highest:

- personal recognition for a job well done

- a written thank you

- public praise.[10]

Recognition is a means to help employees feel valued. However, as a form of positive reinforcement, recognition isn't always applied that way. Typically in the workplace, the best positive reinforcement employees can expect to receive is a lack of negative reinforcement. In other words, if you didn't get your hand slapped for doing something wrong today, you must have done a good job. But how would you know when no one ever tells you? The reality is many managers are quick to criticize and slow to praise. Even Harvard researchers have documented that we are "stingy" with praise in the workplace.[11]

Managers can have fun with **Recognition**; e.g., sending flowers or a goody basket filled with candy or snacks, springing for pizza at lunch, etc. Ever notice the power of food in an office? Bring in delectable treats and you can set off a feeding frenzy!

Companies have become creative in encouraging employee **Recognition.** Managers at Richmond, VA-based Ukrop's Supermarkets™ get special "Thank-You Kits" to use for staff recognition. These kits include thank-you notes and money the managers can use to reward staff with movie tickets, flowers and other tokens of appreciation.[12] McDonald's® Corporation offers its managers and franchisees a line of customized greeting cards they can use to acknowledge their employees' efforts.

Eat'n Park®, a Pittsburgh-based regional chain of family restaurants, developed "The SUPER BOOK" of recognition ideas for its managers with "SUPER ways to keep SUPER employees feeling SUPER about their jobs." I had the opportunity to read a copy of this book when I worked on a consulting project for Eat'n Park®. Along with suggestions for formal recognition, the book includes a number of no-cost and low-cost ideas used by its managers. For example, the management team at one of its restaurants calls the parents of its teenage employees to share appreciation for the employees' good performance.

In my former career in banking, I had the opportunity to witness a powerful example of **Recognition**. Based on the results of a customer satisfaction survey, the bank rewarded the top scoring branch with a special breakfast served by senior management. Instead of just authorizing the branch manager to buy breakfast for the staff, the executive management team brought in and served the morning meal. The bank president poured the juice, the senior vice president of branch administration sliced the bagels, and the head of marketing served the coffee. This special event, which the branch staff enjoyed and talked about with pride for months, was a visible demonstration of management's strong commitment to customers and staff.

According to Jon R. Katzenbach, author of *Why Pride Matters More than Money*, such highly visible recognition events and celebrations are an integral part of how organizations instill pride in performance and contribute to an emotionally committed workforce.[13] The authors of *Firms of Endearment* echo the value of recognition: "Yes, a high salary and generous stock options may keep an employee on the payroll, but absent recognition and appreciation, the person will not be bonded with the company. Being unbonded, the employee will not give the company his or her best efforts."[14]

It's easy to dismiss **Respect** and **Recognition** as fluff, but they are critical to engaging employees. You can find evidence of both in the following questions developed by the Gallup Organization to determine the strength of the workplace:

- Do I know what is expected of me at work? **[Respect]**

- Do I have the materials and equipment I need to do my work right? **[Respect]**

- In the last seven days, have I received recognition or praise for doing good work? **[Recognition]**

31

- Is there someone at work who encourages my development? [Respect]

- This last year, have I had opportunities at work to learn and grow?[15] [Respect]

These are five of twelve powerful questions that Gallup discovered have strong links to one or more of the following business outcomes: employee productivity, retention, customer satisfaction and profitability.[16]

Reinforcement: Continually Supporting a Customer-Focused Culture

The 3rd R of gaining employee commitment — **Reinforcement** — allows you to continually support a customer-focused message in both word and deed. In almost all your internal written and verbal communications, you have the opportunity to reinforce the importance of taking care of customers: in staff memos and newsletters (print and electronic), bulletin boards (yes, they're still out there), signage, staff meetings, special events, etc.

Here are examples of what some organizations in the private and public sector have done to reinforce a customer-focused culture:

- In an MBNA® credit card service center (before its acquisition by Bank of America®), the words "Think Like the Customer" were painted over each doorway as reminders of the importance of being empathetic with customers.

- At QVC®, the cable shopping network, the words "Customer-Focus: Exceeding the Expectations of Every Customer" are inlaid in the atrium floor of its headquarters building.[17]

- Southwest Airlines® encouraged its employees to share their stories of "positively outrageous service" and published them for internal distribution.[18]

- The U. S. Census Bureau celebrates "Customer Service Week" every year in early October as part of a national effort recognizing the importance of customer service. I learned about this first hand when I was invited to participate in their festivities. They celebrate with a range of activities including presentations by special guest speakers, exhibits where staff can vote on the most customer-focused displays, and a program book filled with customer service success stories from both customers and employees. One year they even developed a customized game that reinforced the importance of customer service.

When it comes to **Reinforcement**, the most powerful message comes from managers whose actions demonstrate the importance of being attentive and responsive to customers. Employees pay close attention to the cues provided by their managers, and they are quick to ascertain the difference between lip service and true commitment to customers. For example, managers who shy away from customers cannot expect their staff to go the extra mile in providing customer care. Any printed or verbal reinforcement will be rendered ineffective if managers do not "walk the talk."

The 3 Rs Formula for gaining employee commitment — **Respecting your employees, Recognizing their efforts, and Reinforcing the importance of their being customer-focused** — is the foundation of an effective internal marketing strategy. We'll continue to see evidence of these 3 Rs in the next few chapters as we move from a general framework to specific internal marketing tools you can use to take care of the people who matter most.

Introduction to Action Plan Starter Notes

Now that I've laid the groundwork for internal marketing with the 3 Rs Formula for gaining employee commitment, you can begin the process of building your internal marketing plan by answering the questions on the next two pages. Each set of Action Plan Starter Notes (included here and at the end of the next few chapters) is designed to help you capture your thoughts and ideas as you begin to plan how to implement internal marketing in your organization. At the end of this book, you'll also find special worksheets you can use to compile a summary of your Starter Notes and outline your customized internal marketing action plan.

Instructions:

Take a few minutes to identify how your organization practices each of the Rs in the 3 Rs Formula for gaining employee commitment. List all relevant activities and efforts (current and/or planned) that apply to each question below.

a) How does your organization show **Respect** for employees?

b) How does your organization **Recognize** employees for a job well done?

c) How does your organization **Reinforce** a
   customer-focused culture?

CHAPTER 3

Building a Strong Employee-Customer Connection

Employees ... the most powerful medium for conveying the brand to customers.

Leonard L. Berry and A. Parasuraman [1]

Internal marketing impacts two types of relationships:

1. The relationship between employees and customers.

2. The relationship among employees.

In this chapter we'll look at some of the tools and activities you can use to build the relationship between customers and employees in what I call the **Employee-Customer Link.** We'll also explore how to involve "behind-the-scenes" staff — those people who do not have regular customer contact. As a disclaimer, many of the following examples are drawn from a variety of industries. Some activities you may recognize because you're using them or tried them in the past. In that case, I encourage you to continue the activities that work for you. Other activities may have limited applicability due to the nature of your organization. Where possible, be open to exploring how you may be able to adapt and apply them to your situation.

Customer Relationship Tools for All Employees

Reinforce the "big picture"

As previously mentioned in the 3 Rs, under **Respect**, all employees must know how their jobs fit within the scope of the organization, including how their actions impact customers (whether directly or indirectly). Why is this important? Because customer satisfaction rates can double when employees know what roles their activities play in delivering good service.[2]

A person's respective role in an organization, i.e., where he or she fits in the "big picture," usually gets communicated to new employees through job descriptions and orientation. But what about current employees — when do they get to be reminded of their role and impact in the overall organization? For some it may only be at their annual performance time. In today's on-demand world, where managers spend more time putting out workplace "fires" than practicing organizational fire prevention, it is easy to lose sight of the big picture. The need to reinforce employees' fit in the organization, including reminding them how what they do contributes to customer satisfaction and the bottom line, has never been more important.

This is best communicated in face-to-face meetings with managers, in staff meetings, training sessions, and at special employee events such as employee appreciation days, new product launches, promotional kick-offs, etc.

The "big picture" can also be reinforced in internal media, including employee newsletters and the intranet.

While reinforcing the "big picture" sounds like a no-brainer, it is easily overlooked and has become a challenge for many managers to continually and proactively deal with in light of all their other responsibilities. After orientation, new employees settle into their respective roles to focus more narrowly on the job at hand and may lose sight of the "big picture." Also, as a company grows over time, employees may become disconnected from the organization as a whole. With more layers on the organizational chart and/or more office locations, employees become distanced from corporate management and, as a result, tend to associate more with the particular office or division where they work (i.e., proximity breeds familiarity).

Here is an example of this situation from higher education:

A university administrator was leaving his office one day when he came across a prospective student and his parents wandering around campus. They asked for help in finding a particular building, but the administrator did not know where the building was — although he had worked at the school for 20 years! This "AHA" moment led the administrator to discover that due to the school's large size, complexity, and silo mentality, most of the university staff lacked a campus-wide perspective. In other words, employees spent most of their time working within a single building on campus, with the same faculty and/or staff members.[3]

To remedy this situation, the administrator launched a university "ambassador" program to better familiarize staff with the many facets of the institution and its operation. This approach was modeled after a community leadership program. Selected groups of employees participated in a year-long curriculum that provided hands-on learning about the university's major divisions. The program also included a professional development component focused on improving communication, collaboration, and customer service. The underlying premise was that the more staff knew about the school's inner workings, the more connected they became, and the more likely they were to take ownership of the school's mission.[4]

Share customer information

Inherent in the **Employee-Customer Link** is the basic premise that employees know and understand who your customers are and what is important to them. Employees should also be aware of what competitive choices your customers and prospects have, why they choose to do business with you, as well as what they think of your organization and its competitors.

Basic customer data that can be shared includes customer profiles, results of customer satisfaction studies, complaint tracking, and general customer feedback. Excluding proprietary and sensitive data, as much customer information as possible should be circulated throughout the organization. This information should not just be limited to marketing, sales, or call center staff.

The more knowledgeable your employees are about customers, the better they can serve those customers.

Involve employees in improving customer satisfaction

Successful high-tech entrepreneur Andrew Filipowski said it best: "The insiders of an organization understand the stupidity of its traditions better than the outsiders."[5]

When you share the results of customer satisfaction surveys internally, ask employees for their input on what barriers get in the way of satisfying customers or delivering on the brand promise. Also ask for their ideas on how to get around such roadblocks. You can elicit important insight when you pose this question to employees: "If you were leading this organization, what change(s) would you make to improve customer satisfaction?" The key is to ask — employees can be a valuable source of improvement ideas — then listen and respond appropriately.

In their study of customer-engaged organizations, researchers William Band and John Guaspari share an example of an insurance company with a unique approach to employee involvement in customer satisfaction. The company organized a team of 15 employees representing all areas of the organization to conduct face-to-face interviews with a broad range of customers. This team compiled and synthesized the results into a "customer value guide" they then shared with all employees. They also developed a half-day

43

workshop designed to help each employee answer two key questions:

1. Why do customers buy from us rather than our competition?

2. How does my work and my attitude each day affect the likelihood of that happening?

As a result of these "value conversations," employees at the insurance company improved a critical process that positively impacted customer satisfaction and other key profitability measures.[6]

Conduct an 'Open House' inviting customers to connect with staff

Most companies communicate with their customers primarily through e-mail, regular mail, and phone. With increasing time constraints, as technology allows for more convenient and expedient communication, we are seeing a decline in one of the richest forms of communication — face-to-face. Beyond direct sales interactions, what other opportunities do companies have to interact with their customers, in-person?

Look at how these companies create those opportunities:

- Quad/Graphics®, a Wisconsin-based printing company, invites customers to attend a three day "camp" that consists of a mix of educational seminars and fun events. Besides helping customers become more educated buyers of printing services, the event brings customers and staff together to forge a stronger bond with the company. [7]

- Chrysler® sponsors recreational events (Camp Jeep®, Jeep® 101, and Jeep® Jubilee) that teach and promote off-road driving. These events also provide opportunities for Chrysler® engineers to connect with customers. [8]

- The staff of the Lehigh University® Office of Distance Education works hard to make connections with its clients. In addition to its online course offerings, Lehigh partners with companies throughout the U.S. to provide their employees with graduate education studies via satellite broadcast. In the early years of its satellite operation, Lehigh hosted a special forum for its Site Coordinators, the corporate contacts responsible for administering the University's programs at their respective companies. The half-day event included a tour of campus and satellite classrooms; a special panel discussion with Distance Education faculty and staff (broadcast live by satellite to allow participation by those Site Coordinators unable to travel to campus that day); and a luncheon where the Site Coordinators networked with faculty, administration, technical staff, and other company coordinators. According to Peg Portz, Distance Education Program Manager, "Our programs may be by distance, but not our relationships."

If hosting such recreational/educational events may not be practical, consider a simple open house where you invite customers to your place of business to meet and mingle with staff. You can open such an activity to all your customers or do it on a more selected basis, depending on your situation. Employees can serve as "hosts" and conduct tours, if appropriate.

If your company's physical layout does not allow for an on-site event, consider hosting a social get-together at another venue, such as a restaurant or club. Regardless of the type and location of event, remember the main purpose is to connect staff and customers. This may be the only opportunity they have to meet in person. When it comes to building customer rapport and relationships, there is tremendous value in enabling both customers and staff to see the face of someone they previously only knew by name or voice.

Mystery shop your business

Where appropriate, depending on your industry or type of business, staff may be able to act as customers to simulate a consumer's experience with your competitors. For example, a catalog company may have its employees do business with another catalog company so they can experience what it is like to call for information, place an order, receive it, and even evaluate what is involved in canceling the order or returning the item purchased.[9]

Mystery shopping provides empathy for the customer's experience along with critical insight on what is needed to improve one's own operations in comparison. If this activity is not appropriate to do with your competitors, consider mystery shopping in-house, where you call around your own organization as a customer or prospect looking for information on your company's products and services. Ask participating employees to evaluate how they were treated during the call. Have them rate how accurate the information provided was to their issue and how responsive the employee providing the information was to their expressed need. This type of exercise is valuable in helping staff gain a better perspective on what kinds of experiences consumers have when doing business with you.

These tools — reinforcing the big picture, sharing customer information, involving employees in customer satisfaction improvement, hosting an open house type of event, and mystery shopping — can be used with all employees, not just those who have customer contact. But staff who have limited or no direct contact with customers, especially employees who work behind-the-scenes, pose a unique challenge. Let's explore some ways to link them to the customer.

Customer Relationship Tools for Non-Contact Staff

Herbal tea maker Celestial Seasonings® has a unique approach to making their customer tangible to their employees. They created a composite model in the persona of a woman named Tracy Jones to humanize and better visualize a demographic profile of their ideal consumer. Instead of talking about an invisible mass of consumers who buy their products, Celestial Seasonings®staff find it easier to refer to "Tracy" and her needs.[10]

Here are some other ways to tangibly connect to the customer:

Play "Clue"

This isn't the Milton Bradley® board game that you may have grown up with ("Colonel Mustard in the library with the lead pipe"), but a staff exercise you can do at a department or unit level. First, list all the job functions in your department. Then identify all the "clues" a person in that position has to determine whether a customer is satisfied.

Let's use a restaurant as an example. The job functions in a restaurant include the wait staff, chef, cooks, dishwasher, manager, host/hostess, and cashier. So what clues to customer satisfaction does each person have? For those who are wait staff, the clues are fairly obvious since they have direct, face-to-face contact — they can see it in the customer's body language, verbal complaints or compliments, and the amount of their tip. What about the dishwasher who stays in the kitchen? That person gets to see how much food is left over on the plate as well as hear customer feedback about the restaurant from people who know he or she works there. The key to this exercise (and it can be an eye opener) is that even staff who do not have regular contact with customers are not clueless when it comes to knowing what customers think about you.

Visit customers

Consider these examples of how companies get their behind-the-scenes staff to visit customer sites.

The shop floor employees of a tool and die plant joined the salespeople when they made customer calls. These visits allowed them to actually see how their products are used and helped them receive ideas from end-users on product improvements.[11]

The head of a contract food service management firm would periodically invite new corporate staff (from finance, human resources, information services, etc.) to have lunch with him at one of their client locations: a retirement community dining room, college snack bar, or hospital cafeteria. These lunches gave corporate staff the opportunity to experience the company's service from a customer's perspective and, at the same time, connect with the company's field staff: the food service directors, cooks, and servers, who are their colleagues and/or internal customers.

Adopt-a-customer

One of the food service directors from this same company shared the following story.

He had been assigned to manage the food service at a nursing home, which was a newly acquired account for his company. To improve both client and employee satisfaction, the food service director implemented an "adopt-a-resident" program where staff who prepared and assembled meal trays were allowed to spend time each week interacting with one of the residents. As a result of getting to know their customers better, food workers exerted more attention and pride in preparing their meals. So, instead of assembling a low salt, low sugar meal for "the diabetic in room 1123," the work became more personal: "Here's Marie's lunch for today." This program also improved client satisfaction.

Another example comes from a telecommunications company that used non-sales employees to serve as account ambassadors. These employees visited accounts on a quarterly basis, "putting a face on the company" and letting customers know that the company cared about them. What made this program unusual was the fact that employees volunteered for the opportunity to meet customers face-to-face. The ambassador program was successful in contributing both to stronger employee development and improved customer retention.[12]

Conduct customer roundtables

Inviting select groups of customers to meet with you and share their ideas is a great relationship-building and research tool. If you host a customer roundtable, consider inviting a few non-contact staff to observe the session so they can hear the "voice of the customer" firsthand.

Be aware there are two caveats to using this approach successfully:

1. That customers must not be inhibited or intimidated by having staff observe their roundtable session.

2. That employees who observe should listen quietly without getting defensive or overreacting to any negative customer feedback.

These concerns can be managed with careful consideration of and communication with the parties involved. With the cooperation of both participating customers and staff, customer roundtables can be an effective tool to facilitate customer understanding by non-contact staff.

What if having employees involved as direct observers is not feasible? As part of their internal marketing efforts, Reading, PA-based manufacturer, Carpenter Technology Corporation™, organized and videotaped a series of presentations given by major customers to groups of employees. The videotapes were then shown to the rest of employees so they could better understand what was important to their customers.[13]

The key to these tools is to make a tangible connection to the customer — to have non-contact employees see customers as real people rather than faceless names or account numbers. Although the methods organizations use to build these linkages may differ, the benefits are the same:

- Employees develop a better awareness and understanding of customers.

- Staff feel more valued as part of the company's team, gaining insight and developing empathy for fellow staff members that have customer contact.

- As a result of being connected to the customer in a tangible way, employees strengthen their commitment to serving customers.

What will work best for you in linking non-contact employees with customers will depend on your situation. But, used effectively, these internal marketing tools enable all employees, regardless of their level of customer-contact, to sharpen their customer-focus and make stronger connections to customers.

Action Plan Starter Notes

Instructions:

List how your organization connects employees with customers. If applicable, specify any differences for customer contact and non-contact staff.

a) All employees

b) Customer contact employees

c) Non-customer contact employees

CHAPTER 4

Strengthening the Internal Service Culture

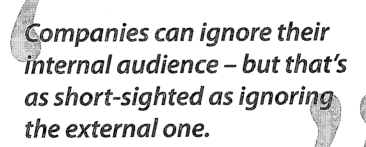

"Companies can ignore their internal audience – but that's as short-sighted as ignoring the external one.

William J. McEwen[1]

In the previous chapter, *Building a Strong Employee-Customer Connection,* I described the internal marketing tools that can strengthen the relationship between employees and customers. This chapter deals with the tools managers can use to strengthen the relationship among employees, including those who are "internal customers." Internal customers are employees whose job functions depend on other employees. For example, managers who need to hire staff or who need help with supervisory training are considered internal customers of Human Resources and Training and Development. A department head who needs a special data report is an internal customer of Information Services.

It should be no surprise that the way people treat each other within an organization impacts how they ultimately treat external customers. In organizations where employees take care of each others' business service needs, they tend to do even better with external customers. In other words, good internal service drives good external customer service.

To strengthen employee relationships, we need to view the **Internal Service Culture** of an organization. Culture is reflected through "the attitudes, behaviors, belief systems, commitments, values, decision-making processes, innovation and productivity that impact the long-term, as well as day-to-day, performance of the business."[2] Companies with strong service cultures are both customer- and employee-focused.

According to Dr. Jerome Want, a partner at Organization Strategies International and author of *Corporate Culture: Eliminating the Black Hole,* "Companies with service cultures focus on fulfilling the customer's needs first, in order to serve their own. Mission, strategy, structure, systems, policies and operations all start and end with the customer ... Companies with true service cultures recognize that the employee is the critical link between the company and its customers."[3]

An example of an organization with a strong service culture is The Container Store®, a successful retail operation that "maintains it must astonish its employees with great treatment before it can expect them to do the same for customers."[4] The company's culture is cited in a research study on "The Empathetic Organization" that found "a stunning 97% of employees agree with the survey statement 'People care about each other here.'"The Container Store®'s positive culture contributes to high employee retention — it has a turnover rate of 28% for salespeople, compared with the industry average of over 73%.[5]

The success of Southwest Airlines® has also been attributed to its service culture and values. It's not just customers who need to be well served – an employee who mistreats another employee can be fired. The rationale is, "If you don't treat your co-workers well, you aren't going to treat the customer well."[6]

It's What's Inside that Counts

What do your employees think of your organization? Here's a simple way to assess your firm's internal service culture; ask this question: Would you refer a friend to work here? It is a loaded question, but the answer will provide you with tremendous insight into the mindset of the employees in your organization.

Following are the key internal marketing components needed to create and support a strong **Internal Service Culture**. These involve having a shared, well-understood mission; a solid employee orientation program; strong internal support and appreciation; and effective internal communications.

Shared mission/vision

According to Gallup research, "if a company wants to harness the power of its workforce, its employees must have a crystal-clear understanding of exactly what the company expects from each of them."[7] So we're back to the employee's role in the "big picture," but with a slightly different context this time. Here the focus is on explaining what is expected of employees — working individually and as a team — in fulfilling the mission.

59

Try this interesting experiment sometime: if you were to randomly approach employees and ask them to repeat the company's mission, how many would be able to repeat it? Of those who could repeat it, how many would then be able to explain what it means?

Awareness of the corporate mission and ability to recite it are not enough. While most mission statements are beautifully crafted, they are not easy to relate to. Most statements couldn't pass what I call the "that's-nice-but-what-does-it-really-mean?" test. Mission statements abound that promise ... "to be the best" ... "to provide customer value"... and "to exceed customer expectations"— but what do these phrases really mean? As good as these terms sound, they are relative and abstract. A mission statement is not meaningful unless it is made real and applicable, which involves translating the mission into specific, measurable behaviors.

For example, assume you have been hired as a teller by the Friendliest National Bank. At orientation you are told: "Welcome to the Friendliest National Bank, where our name is our motto." (Where have you heard that before?) But at this orientation the bank goes one step further to explain the mission in terms of its expectations, and you are told the following:

Being a teller at the Friendliest National Bank means:

- You welcome all customers at your window with a smile and appropriate greeting *("good morning" or "good afternoon")*.

- You use the customer's name during the transaction.

- You process each transaction according to established bank standards.

- If time permits, you suggest other bank services that may be helpful to the customer.

- You conclude transactions with a smile, acknowledgment and appropriate close *("thanks for banking with us" . . . "have a great day")*.

Now you know what type of behavior is expected of you as a teller at the Friendliest National Bank.

Here are samples of how other organizations make their mission statements more meaningful:

- The Ritz-Carlton® specifies the behaviors it wants hotel employees to exhibit in providing its "Gold Standard" service. For example: extend a warm and sincere greeting; use the guest's name; anticipate and comply with guest needs; and give guests a fond farewell. These and other more detailed service standards are printed on plastic, wallet-sized cards that all employees carry as part of their uniform.[8]

- Yellow Freight Systems® created a powerful mission that is simple, yet comprehensive: *Pick stuff up on time, deliver it on time, and don't bust it.*[9]

Only when employees clearly understand what is expected of them in fulfilling the mission — when the

61

mission is made real and meaningful — can they start to
internalize it.

Once the mission is made real, the next step is
to use every opportunity to explain it, repeat it, and
demonstrate it in communications with employees. As
mentioned in Chapter 2, most companies have a variety
of internal media available to convey and reinforce the
mission, including employee newsletters, staff meetings,
signage, orientation, and training. A growing trend is to
use employee identification tags for this purpose. General
Motors'® Saturn division and eBay® are two of the
companies that distribute laminated cards printed with
their mission, vision, and values to employees to wear
alongside their corporate ID badges.[10]

More than just creating awareness, however, internal
marketing should be used to take the mission beyond
a mere statement and maximize its effectiveness as a
dynamic guide for how the company operates and what
employees are expected to do. This means finding ways
to:

1. Share information on how to live up to the mission.

2. Recognize employees who are successful in
   providing outstanding service to customers
   and each other, including positioning such
   staff as role models (Marketing Heroes, Brand
   Champions, etc.).

New employee orientation

Remember your first day in a new job? Remember how you felt in the following weeks? Making a good first impression is important for both the new employee *and* the company. From the company's perspective, how are new employees introduced and welcomed to your organization? How do they learn your culture and values?

Starbucks® CEO Howard Schultz greets all new hires via video, where he shares the company's history and culture, what it stands for, and what they are trying to achieve in what he calls the "imprinting period of the new employee."[11] It is during this critical "imprinting period" that new employees get to see the "big picture" perspective for the first time, including where they fit in and how they can contribute to the organization's goals.

The importance of an effective orientation program cannot be overstated. "By developing an effective, comprehensive orientation program, organizations can both speed up cultural learning and send a message to new employees that the organizations genuinely care for these employees and are doing all that they can to ensure success ..."[12]

Welcoming and bonding activities are critical at both the organizational and departmental (or other sub-unit) level. According to Nancy Alrichs, author of *Competing for Talent*, "New hires should feel welcome and confident that they will succeed ... and that they have made the right decision . . . The personal touch is also needed within the department, between the new hire and his or her co-workers and between the supervisor and the new hire. If no one cares enough to make new people feel welcome, how can the organization expect them to care about staying?"[13]

At Eat'n Park®, the Pittsburgh-based restaurant chain, the job of welcoming employees is shared by both corporate staff (who run orientation) and the individual restaurant where the new employee is assigned. Before orientation, the local restaurant manager circulates a "Welcome to the Team" card for the staff to sign. The manager includes a note with the new team member's name, position, and a fun fact about the person (such as his/her hobbies, unique talents, pets, etc.) to encourage communication between the new hire and the existing staff. The card is then presented to the new hire when that person joins the team. This approach not only makes the new employee feel more welcome, it helps reduce the anxiety among current staff about the new team member.

Such welcoming and orientation-related activities facilitate the bonding process and can reinforce a good fit between new employee and employer. An effective orientation program can also favorably impact short-term employee retention. Corning Glass® found employees who went through a positive orientation were 69% more likely to be with the company three years later.[14]

Internal support and appreciation

For an organization to sustain a strong service culture, it must recognize and reinforce the "internal customer" concept — employees serving other employees who serve the customer.

One effective way to demonstrate the importance of internal support is by trading places or role switching:

- Once a year, corporate employees at Applebee's Neighborhood Bar and Grill® work a shift at one of their restaurants. CEO Lloyd Hill shared what he learned when he did his shift as a busboy. "I learned that every person is very important. If we don't have great dishwashers, then we can't serve you your meal — and then having the best food, the lowest prices, and the friendliest staff means nothing."[15]

- At UPS®, sales representatives go out with the drivers on their delivery runs; the drivers will also accompany the sales reps on sales calls. The sales reps gain a better perspective of what is involved in delivering packages, whereas the drivers gain a better appreciation of what is involved in getting the business.

- A major hotel chain participates in an "In-Touch" day where corporate staff goes into the field to work at different hotel properties. A marketing executive may work a shift with the bell captain; an internal auditor or accountant might work in housekeeping; and an information systems specialist may work in the kitchen or laundry area.[16]

The value of trading places is that it can help build empathy for the frontline and reinforce teamwork and a sense of common purpose. In other words, it sends the message *"We're all in this together."*

Strong support also comes from top management who lead by example. In both word and deed, managers have the opportunity to communicate and reinforce the company's commitment to customers. "Leadership behavior sends the strongest message," according to Lawrence A. Crosby and Sheree L. Johnson, specialists in loyalty research. "Many people in top leadership positions have become detached from the day-to-day business of their company. Their leadership behaviors may be uninformed and therefore ineffective."[17]

To remedy this situation, leaders need to connect with their employees *and* customers.

Here are several examples of how senior executives can make these connections and demonstrate their commitment to both internal and external customers:

- The president of a credit union works as a teller for a day so he can spend more time with customers and frontline employees.

- At a large regional bank undergoing a merger, employees were invited to "chat with the chairman" on a designated employee hotline. Both the chairman and president also spent time taking groups of employees to lunch to discuss staff concerns and ideas.

- Once a year at ServiceMaster®, a company that provides cleaning and support services to hospitals, schools, and industrial firms, top management will clean hospital operating rooms and customers' toilets to show their support for frontline employees.[18]

Such experiences help build empathy by reminding executives what it is like to be on the frontline. And in receiving management's attention, employees feel more valued. Any effort that brings top management closer to employees also helps strengthen teamwork and a shared customer-focused orientation. As Crosby and Johnson have consistently found in their research, "leadership is one of the critical paths to building employee commitment."[19]

Internal support can also be reinforced through special recognition. One such example is Marriott®'s Hospitality Gold Star Program created by one of their vacation resort properties. Each week three guests are randomly selected and asked to identify the hotel associate they found most helpful. These associates get a gold star to wear on their uniform, along with a monetary award; the guests are also rewarded with a gift for their participation. But the program doesn't stop there. Staff, who have been recognized by the guests, are then asked to identify three associates from the "heart of the house" (i.e., those behind the scenes) who were most helpful to them. These internal associates also receive a gold star and monetary award.[20] This program is truly a win-win-win situation.

As previously mentioned in the **3 R's** (Chapter 2), recognition has great motivational and pride-instilling value. But management does not have to wait for displays of special or extraordinary effort before they apply recognition. For example, Marriott® conducts a week long, company-wide event for Associate Appreciation that includes "parties, contests, special rewards and a lot of heartfelt thanking" to "remind everyone in Marriott® on the same day, at the same time, that we're all in this adventure together."[21]

In its "SUPER BOOK" of team recognition ideas, Eat'n Park® encourages its restaurant managers to host "Smile-abrations." These include hosting a special buffet to recognize teamwork or celebrating the major holidays with special treats for employees: a management-made green milkshake on St. Patrick's Day; red, white and blue Popsicles on July 4th; and trick-or-treat bags for Halloween.

Effective internal communications

Last, but certainly not least, we come to the importance of communications. To be effective within an organization, communication needs to travel openly in all directions:

↓ top-down (from senior management to all employees)

↑ bottom-up (from all levels of employees back up to senior management)

⇄ laterally (across all levels of the organization).

As previously mentioned, customer profiles and the results of customer satisfaction research should be shared using top-down and lateral channels to enable employees to better understand who their customers are and how these customers feel about the company. In the bottom-up channel, employees can be asked to share any feedback they get from customers; they can also provide input on how to improve products, services, and customer care.

Despite the importance of bottom-up and lateral communications for employee involvement, these channels are not always used effectively in organizations. If you want to encourage more bottom-up communications, consider the impact of your top-down channel. One study I read found 70% of employees are afraid to speak up or ask for clarification for fear of being rejected or chastised.[22] The principle of "no pain, no gain" does little to motivate employees to contribute their ideas to the company.

To encourage more bottom-up communications, companies are using creative formats such as informal "fireside chats" or "town hall" type meetings with management.[23] Some larger firms even host executive management "talk shows" broadcast throughout their organizations. These corporate talk shows can be set up primarily for information-sharing purposes, not the mud-slinging format of shock-value talk shows.[24]

Note: The need for effective internal communications is not limited to large firms; smaller organizations have their own challenges. Although their size seems to be an advantage in that they have fewer people to get the message to, the issue for small organizations is that internal communications may be taken for granted because it is assumed to take place.

In the lateral or horizontal dimension of communications, another study found overall employee dissatisfaction with communications, both between and within departments.[25] This is not surprising given the silo mentality of departments within organizations; for example, operations doesn't talk to accounting, accounting doesn't talk to marketing, marketing doesn't talk to information systems, and so on. The resulting silence leads to situations where the left hand doesn't know what the right hand is doing, and it can cost them dearly (A case in point is NASA's costly and "humiliating" mistake that destroyed the multi-million dollar Mars Climate Orbiter. Engineers involved in the project used different numbers for its navigation: one group used English units while another group assumed the figures were metric.[26])

It is important for individual departments or business units to take the time to communicate what is happening in their respective areas, especially when their actions may impact another area of the organization (e.g., inviting representatives from other parts of the business into their departmental staff meeting to share what they are doing). The key is for the company to be proactive in ensuring that internal communications flow openly in all directions so that staff will feel an important link to the rest of the organization.

Regardless of which communications channel we're using, thanks to technology, we can usually communicate easily and efficiently with e-mail. And that has created its own set of challenges:

1. Information overload — we need to be sensitive to the growing amount of information that employees have to absorb on a daily basis.

2. Electronic conversations — while e-mail is an expedient medium, it should not be used as a substitute for personal interaction (especially when geographic proximity is not an issue). Unfortunately, face-to-face communication is suffering as there is a growing over-reliance on e-mail at the expense of regular staff meetings.

Internal marketers need to be sensitive to these concerns as they endeavor to efficiently and effectively communicate with employees without contributing to information overload. The key is to prioritize what critical information is needed — and how can it best be communicated — to engage employees and connect them with customers, fellow employees, and the organization overall.

The tools covered in this and the previous chapter — those that positively impact a firm's **Internal Service Culture** and strengthen the **Employee-Customer Link** — are important components of an internal marketing effort, but they are by no means exhaustive. The magic of internal marketing is that there is no magic. Internal marketing includes any and all programs, events, activities, and internal public relations efforts that reinforce the importance of customers and the employees who take care of them.

71

Action Plan Starter Notes

Instructions:

List what your organization does to strengthen its
Internal Service Culture.

a) Mission/vision

b) Employee orientation

c) Internal collaboration and support

d) Internal communications

e) Other

CHAPTER 5

Spotlight: At the Heart of Employee-Customer Care

Employees either benefit or burden every dimension of a company's existence. The extent to which they deliver one or the other is primarily a function of company culture and leadership's view of employees' value to the company.

From the book *Firms of Endearment*[1]

N ow that we've reviewed the internal marketing tools you can use to strengthen the employee-customer link and the internal service culture, let's look at how these tools come together to engage employees.

While numerous organizations have been cited throughout the book to illustrate a variety of internal marketing activities, this chapter spotlights one company to provide a more comprehensive picture of how internal marketing can be seamlessly applied. The company is a former client of mine, for whom I had the privilege of working as a training consultant for several years. I witnessed first hand its commitment to employee and customer care.

Meet Wood Dining Services, a contract food service management firm based in eastern Pennsylvania, that I believe best exemplifies what internal marketing is all about. It was acquired in 2001 by Sodexho Alliance™, a leading food and services management company in North America. Because I am familiar with how Wood Dining Services used internal marketing before Sodexho™

entered the picture, I will showcase the company in its former life.

M. W. "Scotty" Wood was running his own restaurant in the 1940s in Allentown, PA, when he was approached by a nearby college to manage its dining services. Over the next sixty years, he and his son expanded the company to provide contract food service management for educational, healthcare, and business organizations. At its peak (pre-acquisition), Wood Dining Services employed more than 15,000 people serving more than 500 accounts across 28 states, with a 99% client retention rate.[2]

The company's success was based on many things, including its relentless focus on employee-customer care (this was the company referred to in Chapter 3 whose CEO invited new employees to lunch at client sites and whose food service director initiated the adopt-a-customer program at a nursing home).

The following is an expanded description of their internal marketing efforts based on an interview with the founder's son and former CEO, Robert C. Wood, who was committed to maintaining the quality service culture established by his father.

"Our People"

Let's start with the company's vision and mission. Wood Dining Services' vision was "to be the company of choice for our people, our clients, and our vendors." Their mission was "to be the best food and service management company and to grow profitably by pursuing lasting partnerships with our people, customers, clients and suppliers, and by sharing our passion for food service, creativity, and entrepreneurship."

What is most striking is that "our people" tops the list of stakeholders in both the vision and mission. According to Bob Wood, the placement of employees first was deliberate:

"I don't think any of us would be successful without our people. If they can't be successful in their roles, then we won't be successful. It's just so basic to me . . . they chose to work here, they have personal objectives, personal needs. And if we don't fulfill their needs, we're never going to get anywhere.

"To me an employee is a legal term; it's not how we should look at our people. They have kids, they have ambitions, they have goals . . . we want this to be the best job they ever had. Plus we want them to advance and evolve to get better jobs over time . . . So to me, it always starts with our people."

One of the traditions started by his father and continued by Bob was sending birthday cards as an opportunity to acknowledge each employee. On the back of the card was a brief company description that reinforced its culture:

"The Wood Company's recipe for success is developing and nurturing its people. We value and understand the difference they can make in pleasing our customers. We believe in celebrating our people's success and important events in their lives."

Also on the back was a picture of the founder with this quote:

"We hope our caring about you helps you care about making a difference to your fellow staff members and our customers."

This simple act of acknowledging employees' birthdays — a means to recognize everyone at least once a year — reinforced their value to the company and was reflective of its people-oriented culture.

Recognition

Service to clients and internal customers (fellow employees) was highly valued and recognized, both formally and informally. Favorable letters received from clients were posted on a *Wall of Fame* displayed in the halls of the company's home office where it was visible to both employees and visitors. When clients sent letters to Bob commending Wood employees, he followed up by calling the employees to extend his own appreciation. He would then send them a copy of the letter. When the General Managers received such letters, they responded similarly and also sent copies to Bob. He, in turn, responded to the General Managers with a note saying "I'm glad you did this," because Bob recognized the need for reinforcement at all levels of the company.

In addition, if an employee helped Bob with a question or problem, he gave them a signed "Credit Card" about the size of a regular business card that read: Your response to my need is greatly appreciated and you deserve 'credit' for helping me fulfill my responsibilities.

The company also conducted its share of formal recognition activities. Each corporate division held an annual Appreciation Event to recognize salaried staff. When plaques for service were presented, each inscription was read out loud so the acknowledged employees and co-workers understood the reason for the recognition.

What is most telling about the power of recognition is the response Bob received when he was out in the field, where he spent 70% of his time. In his pocket, he carried a handful of hospitality pins in the shape of pineapples, the universal symbol for hospitality that was also a part of the company's logo. Bob gave these pins to staff whenever he caught them doing something right — like going out of their way to take care of a customer or fellow team member.

> "I think these pins cost 47¢, but these people think you gave them a pile of gold. Everyone wants to be part of something . . . everyone wants to feel that they are valued, that they made a difference. To the degree we can celebrate our people, that's our greatest weapon, our greatest tool."

81

Commitment to Employee-Customer Care

An interesting reinforcement of the company's culture was the creation and distribution of its "Employee Manifesto" — a series of I-statements about the organization's values that each employee pledged to uphold. Following are excerpts from this document:

> Wood Dining Services is committed to providing a professional environment where each employee is expected to strive to maximize his or her own potential and to contribute to the success of the organization. In order to achieve this environment, each employee is expected to abide by the following:

- I will focus on doing what's right for my fellow employees and clients – and that will be one of our competitive advantages.

- I will bring trust, respect, appreciation of differences, and a sense of humor to my relationships.

- I will have fun at my job and encourage others to do the same.

- I will ensure that my customers are constantly awestruck with the quality of their entire experience with us.

- I will insist on honesty and integrity at all times — anything else is unthinkable.

- I will act this way . . . even when no one is watching.

"Even when no one is watching" — what a powerful a statement! Can you get your employees to commit to that?

The "L" Word

I chose to spotlight Wood Dining Services in this chapter to give you an idea of how they applied internal marketing for employee-customer care through ordinary, everyday activities rather than extraordinary events. What I learned by working with and observing this company was a powerful lesson in internal marketing, especially given it was something Wood Dining Services did rather intuitively.

Yet, even with as much internal marketing as they did, Bob Wood admitted even more was needed. He recognized that this process involved continual commitment and a daily, integrated effort. "It's easy to put a poster on the wall," he told me, "but it has to be something that we live." Clearly, Bob and his management team understood the value of internal marketing as an ongoing philosophy, not just a program.

As you probably figured out by now, the key ingredient in internal marketing is **Leadership** – it takes **Leaders** who genuinely care about their customers and the people (employees) who serve them. It takes **Leaders** whose core values recognize that both groups matter

83

and who integrate these values in their culture and operations.

Recent research confirms leadership involvement is critical to internal marketing success. In its 2006 Internal Marketing Best Practices study, the Forum for People Performance Management and Measurement identified six key characteristics that drive successful internal marketing programs:

1. **Senior management participation** and buy-in with visible support and frequent and direct communication from c-level executives.

2. An **integrated organizational structure** to encompass communications with all employees to maximize their involvement and commitment.

3. A formal **strategic internal marketing approach** similar to that applied in external marketing.

4. **Partnership with Human Resources** and its involvement with staff recruitment, retention, training, and internal communications.

5. A **focus on employee engagement** to create a collaborative work environment where employees feel involved.

6. Consistent **internal brand communications** to convey the brand promise to employees and motivate them to deliver on the promise.[3]

Leaders who "get it" know customer relations mirror employee relations — the way their employees feel is the way their customers will feel. So they use internal marketing to send these positive mirror messages:

- When we tell our staff: *We want you to know what's happening in the organization,* the staff tells our customers: *Because I know what's going on, I can help you.*

- When we tell staff: *Here's what you need to know about our customers,* staff tells customers: *Because I know what's important to you, I can take better care of you.*

- When we tell staff: *We want to give you the tools you need to do your job,* staff tells customers: *Because this company cares about me, I care about helping you.*

In organizations with true leadership, "employees as assets" is not just management rhetoric.

CHAPTER 6

Do Happy Employees Ensure Happy Customers?

Answers to These and Other Critical Questions

Happiness in the workplace is a strategic advantage. Service comes from the heart, and people who feel cared for will care more.

Hal G. Rosenbluth[1]

A t this point, with an understanding of why internal marketing is necessary and how it can help you strengthen employee-customer care, it's time to address the potential resistance you may encounter when initiating internal marketing in your organization. In particular, I want to address the critical questions you may be asked and provide you with responses and strategies that will help you overcome these objections.

Critical Question #1

Throughout this book, we've seen numerous evidence of the self-reinforcing relationship between employee- and customer satisfaction. Yet many managers, including the cynics, will still ask: *Do happy employees ensure happy customers?*

Answer: The happy employees = happy customers equation is oversimplified, but how can you have one without the other? This logic is underscored by Hal F. Rosenbluth, head of Rosenbluth® Travel and author of the book *The Customer Comes Second,* in his quote at the beginning of this chapter. Don Silvensky, CEO of

MicroTek Computer Labs®, echoes this philosophy: "If people are happy, they enjoy taking care of customers … It's not a chore."[2] Ditto for Carol Sturman, President of Sturman™ Industries: "Part of our leadership culture is tapping into people's passion and spirit, and giving them something that they can really believe in. If you tap into their hearts and their spirit and their passion, they can do much more than if it's just a job."[3]

On the flip side, consider the impact of unhappy employees. Customers can tell whether an organization is sincere about being customer-focused or whether it's just giving them lip service. They are also quick to pick up on signals of employee satisfaction or dissatisfaction, whether conveyed inadvertently or deliberately.

Here's an example from my own experience. I was enticed to open an account with a new bank that came into my local market, and it was not because of the new account premium. (Seriously, I didn't need any more small kitchen appliances.) Given the bank's reputation for stellar service, as well as its branch office availability seven days a week, I had high expectations. All was well until the day I went to make a withdrawal and the teller slapped the money on the counter when she completed my transaction. Given her facial scowl and limited eye contact that was focused on the paper transaction in front of her, I surmised the teller was having a bad day. However, that's no excuse for her rude behavior.

I had a second less-than-satisfactory encounter with another teller a few weeks later. My expectations about the bank's brand promise unfulfilled, I closed out my account and took my money to another bank.

Bad attitude is just one contributor to a negative encounter. Think about your own experience as a customer dealing with:

- Employees who genuinely want to help customers but are hampered by a lack of internal support.

- Employees who lack the organizational or product knowledge to sufficiently serve customers.

- Employees who are not clued-in to what is going on in the organization, including not knowing the messages or promises that have been communicated to key customer groups or the market-at-large.

- A revolving door of new employees stemming from high turnover (rather than organizational growth).

Experience with one or more of these situations can reflect negatively on an organization and put it at risk for customer dissatisfaction, lost business, and brand damage. As Silvensky says, "People who feel frustrated and powerless will not serve customers well."[4]

Some managers need a reminder and/or reassurance about the link between employee- and customer satisfaction/dissatisfaction. For others, however, the issue becomes another way of asking "Why do we need internal marketing?"

Cynics who still don't buy in to the importance of being employee-focused, in order to be customer-focused, need to be reminded of the negative consequences of ignoring the employee-customer connection. Remember, if your employees don't feel valued, neither will your customers. According to Rosenbluth, "Unhappiness results in error, turnover, and other evils." [5]

In addition to the high cost of employee turnover, customer churn also carries costs to a company's bottom line and reputation. Unhappy customers are not only capable of taking their business away from you, they may harm your existing and potential business by publicly airing and sharing their complaints. Numerous complaint studies have found that dissatisfied consumers will tell five to ten (or more) people about their negative experience, while satisfied consumers share their positive experience with only three to five people.[6] Disgruntled customers are motivated to initiate their negative word-of-mouth campaigns as a form of retribution.[7]

What is truly frightening is that angry customers can turn into crusaders on a mission — vocal, human megaphones who use every opportunity to express their dissatisfaction and displeasure to others. Consider how this group has been empowered by the Internet and the explosion of consumer generated media — organizations who are not careful could find themselves with a www. yourcompanysucks.com website or blog! Yesterday's word-of-mouth is today's word-of-mouse, and today's upset consumers can reach millions of people with a single click.

Important note: as I've shown in this book, your reputation may be harmed not only by unhappy customers, but by unhappy employees as well.

With so much at stake, can you afford *not* to do internal marketing?

Critical Question #2

It's hard to understand why internal marketing isn't more commonplace — especially given the critical importance of the employee-customer connection. *If managers can leverage employee and customer satisfaction through internal marketing, why don't more organizations do it?*

Answer: One reason involves management's traditional view of employees. As Jeffrey Pfeffer, Professor of Organizational Behavior at the Stanford Graduate School of Business, and author of *The Human Equation: Building Profits by Putting People First*, acknowledges:

"Most managers, if they're being honest with themselves, will admit it: When they look at their people, they see cost ... salaries ... benefits ... overhead. Very few companies look at their people and see assets."[8]

"Everybody knows what to do, but nobody does it ... A lot of companies confuse talk with action. They believe that because they said it (acknowledging the value of their employees), it's actually happened ..."[9]

Another explanation is that organizations may practice internal marketing to some degree without recognizing it. Remember, internal marketing is an umbrella concept that covers a range of communications, educational, and motivational efforts reinforcing the value of customers and employees. While some effort is better than none, a deliberate approach will be more effective in engaging employees.

Critical Question #3

Question #1 addressed the relationship between happy employees and happy customers. Let's take this one step further: *Do happy employees ensure organizational success?*

Answer: My honest answer is . . . it depends. It depends on a lot of factors, such as the utility and value of your company's offering, market demand, and competition, to name just a few. If your organization offers a product or service that doesn't meet market needs and/or has little real (or perceived) value, or if your competitors are doing a much better job at satisfying the market, you probably won't be able to maintain your business for long no matter how happy your employees are.

The answer also depends on your business model. The marketplace can change rapidly, putting pressure even on those firms with happy employees and customers. And some companies with a toxic workplace culture do well in spite of themselves (sad, but true).

So let's get real — sometimes bad things happen to good organizations, and sometimes good things happen to bad organizations. But which type of organization would you prefer to be associated with?

Critical Question #4

If you are in a situation where employee value is given lip service, then it is up to you to be proactive and convince top management of the need for internal marketing. Without it, your organization is at risk. *What do you do if you can't get management's support?*

Answer: Don't give up if you're unable to implement internal marketing throughout your organization. The good news is you can still affect change at a micro level — such as within your own department or sub-unit — despite management. I know because I was in this situation.

I once used internal marketing in a small department of five people who worked in a division of a large organization. The corporate culture was operationally and bottom-line driven, with minimal investment in its employees. Working in this organization was a drastic change for me, having come from a previous employer (in the same industry) with strong employee-customer care values. Yet I was able to utilize the 3 Rs (Respect-Recognition-Reinforcement) with my staff and provide the professional and emotional support they needed to better serve our customers.

As a result, my staff felt good about coming to work every day, despite the organizational culture. Internal marketing worked for me in that situation within the confines of my small department.

The benefits of internal marketing can also be leveraged to create a halo effect. Once other managers see your success with internal marketing, they may be more willing to give it a try.

What if management continues to be resistant to your best efforts to apply internal marketing? Then you need to seriously consider your options. The good news is that there are organizations whose values and actions demonstrate genuine commitment to employee-customer care, as evidenced by examples in this book. Remember that you have options — one of which is not to endure working in a toxic culture.

Critical Question #5:

How do I get started with internal marketing?

Answer: Proceed to the next chapter where you'll find a planning checklist, tips for success, and special worksheets based on the concepts in this Guide to Employee-Customer Care. You can use this material, along with your completed Action Plan Starter Notes, to develop your own internal marketing plan.

Action Plan Starter Notes

Instructions:

Respond to the questions below based on your organization's current climate.

a. Describe how your organization views and treats its employees. For example, are they truly valued as assets? Or is it just politically correct to refer to them that way?

b. Based on your response to the above, what is being reflected in your organization's "mirror messages" to your customers? *[Note: Sample messages can be found at the end of Chapter 5.]* Are you sending your customers positive, negative or mixed messages?

c. Will you be able to implement internal marketing on a macro (organization-wide) or micro level? If the latter, identify the specific department(s), division(s) and/or business unit(s) where you plan to use internal marketing.

CHAPTER 7

How to Make It Happen — for You, Your Employees, and Your Customers

The true power of running a company, the true power of growing any enterprise, is 5% technology and 95% psychology.

Hatim Tyabi[1]

T hroughout this book you've read about the value of a positive employee-customer connection and encountered a number of ideas on how others have successfully strengthened that connection. Now what do you do? How do you apply this information to effectively engage your employees for strategic advantage?

Whether you are starting from scratch or building on existing efforts, if you follow the step-by-step checklist I've provided in this chapter, it will help guide you in developing an internal marketing plan that fits your organization. In addition, I have included tips for success to help you make the most of your internal marketing initiatives. You will also find special worksheets at the end of this chapter that have been designed to help you put everything together to create your own Customized Action Plan for Internal Marketing.

Recommended Checklist for Results

✓ DO YOUR HOMEWORK

You need both customer and employee-related research to help you determine how much internal marketing effort is needed to strengthen the **Employee-Customer Link** and the **Internal Service Culture** in your organization.

A good place to start is with any current customer satisfaction measurement your company may already be using. Look at the results of your customer surveys, complaint tracking, and other sources of customer satisfaction research. What are your customers telling you from their survey responses and general feedback about how well you are taking care of them?

Likewise, review the results of any employee satisfaction surveys for a clearer internal look at how your company is doing. What are employees telling you about your organization and its operation? Unfortunately, many organizations do not proactively engage in tracking employee satisfaction unless there are human resources or morale issues. "The reality in many companies is that they know more about their customers than about their employees ..."[2]

Internal research is needed to learn employee perceptions about the organization. Do employees feel they are getting the tools, support, and information they need to do their jobs? Also, what mechanism do you have in place to obtain their suggestions for improving employee and customer care? As mentioned previously in

Chapter 4, one provocative question that has proven to be successful is, "Would you refer a friend to work here?"

Some additional probing questions that will give you insight into how your employees feel about your organization are:

- Why are you working here rather than another company?

- What would cause you to end your employment here?

- What drives you crazy about working here?[3]

Organizations should have research or feedback vehicles in place to gauge both employee and customer satisfaction, although they may not necessarily connect the results. Check with the staff in marketing, customer service operations, or human resources for any customer and employee research they may have conducted (either formally or informally) through interviews, focus groups, or surveys. If none of this information exists, you will need to do your own research.

If you need outside assistance, you can find reputable market research firms that conduct both customer and employee surveys. (Check out members/suppliers affiliated with the American Marketing Association and the Society for Human Resource Management.) When considering suppliers, look for those who conduct "linkage research" — this type of research integrates internal organizational practices and employee perceptions with outcomes that impact customer satisfaction and the bottom line. Linkage research can also help organizations identify the specific practices or "drivers" of service climate that matter most to their customers.[4]

The results of your research will help you determine what areas of employee and customer satisfaction to address and how much internal marketing is needed. Your research will also help you identify any specific employee groups that may need special attention and/or reinforcement.

✓ SEGMENT EMPLOYEES

Internal marketing can be tailored to different employee groups. You can segment employees in a variety of ways:

- By length of employment (new or long-term)

- Employee role/function (operational, customer-service, finance, information systems, purchasing, etc.)

- Type of customer-contact (frontline or non-contact)

- Employment status (full or part-time)

- Management level (supervisor, middle-management, executive).

Another interesting approach is to segment by employee attitudes. Internal Brand Dimensions LLC identified four distinct employee segments based on their attitudes toward management communications:

- "Tuned out and turned off" — negative, nonparticipating employees who are distrustful of company communications or goals.

104

- "Cynics and critics" — mildly negative and skeptical of company information, this is a borderline group that can become either more negative or more positive, depending on management's actions.

- "Aware and on board" — employees who are regularly involved and probably loyal, but fall just short of being fully committed to the company. This group is also borderline and may need a little more attention to be more positive towards management.

- "Tuned in and turned on" — loyal and involved employees who admire and follow management goals.[5]

With numerous ways to segment employees, which type of segmentation should you use? The answer depends on your situation (based on the results of your research described in the previous step) and organization. For example, if you work in a nonprofit, you may need to include volunteers. If you're in a retail operation with multiple stores, you may need to segment geographically. Choose whatever form of segmentation works best for you.

✓ SET YOUR OBJECTIVES

Your specific internal marketing objectives will also depend on your situation and what you learn from your research. These objectives will vary based on what you want to achieve. For example:

- Improve customer satisfaction and/or retention.

- Improve employee satisfaction and/or reduce turnover.

- Review and/or revise orientation.

- Enhance and/or expand staff training.

- Create or refine service recognition.

- Increase participation in training and/or employee programs.

- Improve internal service or teamwork.

If you find you are overwhelmed with multiple objectives, don't panic. Prioritize or rank your objectives based on your organizational needs, then select the top two or three objectives that are most critical. Later on, as the situation improves, you can take stock and decide if it is appropriate to attempt additional objectives. In my experience, I've found organizations are more effective when they focus their efforts on a few priorities instead of trying to accomplish everything at once.

✓ DEVELOP YOUR RESULTING ACTION PLAN

In this step you establish and implement specific internal marketing activities that will enable you to achieve your objectives. Your Action Plan can involve one or more of the following:

- Internal Media and Public Relations — as mentioned throughout the book, there are a number of internal media vehicles you can use to reinforce customer-focused values and recognize employee success stories in serving customers (including, but not limited to, staff newsletters and publications, signage, the intranet, staff ID badges). For example, you can post customer letters on an employee Wall or Hall of Fame, profile customer service "heroes" or "brand ambassadors" in internal publications.

- Special Events — these can include customer or employee appreciation dinners, staff development retreats, special orientation or training programs, and Customer Service Weeks.

- Activities that strengthen the *Employee-Customer Link* (see Chapter 3).

- Activities that strengthen and support the *Internal Service Culture* (see Chapter 4).

✓ MEASURE AND FINE TUNE

This is where you evaluate your efforts relative to your objectives. You can measure the results of specific internal marketing activities and programs quantitatively (based on participation levels, changes in customer and employee satisfaction) and/or qualitatively (via feedback from staff and customers). Monitoring the results of your efforts will tell you how much fine-tuning and adapting is needed.

With this basic checklist, you can easily build an internal marketing initiative.

107

Making It Happen-Tips For Success

Here are several suggestions to help you maximize your internal marketing.

1. Get others involved. Enlist the involvement of Human Resources, Marketing, Operations, Sales, Information Systems, and other important internal allies in this effort. Your goal should be to get other managers to buy-in to the habit of proactively communicating with, educating, and motivating employees. The more you involve others in your organization, the more effective your internal marketing will be.

2. Keep the planning process simple. Consider holding a special staff meeting or mini-retreat to develop your internal marketing strategy and plan, and build some fun into the process. Go off-site (if you can manage it time- and budget-wise) or seclude yourself in a conference room for a half day, full day, or series of half days, depending on how long you think you will need. And don't forget to bring in refreshments to provide those involved with breakfast, lunch, or whatever favorite food will help fuel the planning process.

In your planning session, build discussion around a summary of your **Action Plan Starter Notes** (Worksheet #1, at the end of the chapter, is provided for this purpose), or you can start with a S-W-O-T analysis in which you identify and discuss the Strengths, Weaknesses, Opportunities, and Threats of your company's internal culture and its employee-customer care practices. Once you assess your situation, you'll have a better idea of what needs to be done to move forward, and you can fill-in-the-blanks in your action plan checklist (outlined in Worksheet #2).

The following worksheets can be used as guides to help you organize and develop your internal marketing. Because every organization's situation is unique, I encourage you to adapt the planning tools and approach that work best for you. For example, I've had several clients who chose to focus first on improving their internal communications before addressing their customer satisfaction issues.

However you set it up, you do not need an extensive formal planning effort that results in a four-inch binder that sits on a bookshelf to collect dust. It doesn't matter if you sketch out your internal marketing ideas on a paper placemat at lunch or on a cocktail napkin over drinks, as long as it's something you'll use. I'm a strong believer in keeping it simple so that the people involved in developing your internal marketing plan don't feel overwhelmed.

It's also important to reinforce the positive impact your planning group's efforts will have on co-workers and customers. After all, that's what internal marketing is all about. In one planning session, the facilitator distributed little pocket mirrors to remind the participants that what they see in the mirror is what their customers will see.

3.   **Introduce internal marketing carefully.** Internal marketing is most effective when done gradually or in small doses across an organization. If you implement it as a major new initiative with a lot of fanfare (like Moses coming down the mountain with the Ten

Commandments), you run the risk of it being viewed as another "program-of-the-month." If presented this way, employees are likely to give it cursory acceptance while waiting for the company to jump on the next popular management bandwagon. Given its critical function, internal marketing should never be treated as a management fad du jour.

4. **Focus your impact.** Remember, if you are unable to effect a change in attitude at a macro level, you can still have an impact at a micro level by applying internal marketing within your own department, division, or business unit. If the organizational culture continues to be resistant despite these efforts, you may want to consider your options. One option is to change companies. As you've seen here, there are other organizations whose core values recognize the importance of both customers and employees.

Putting It All Together — Your Customized Action Plan

Now you're ready to develop your Employee-Customer Care Internal Marketing Action Plan using the following worksheets.

As you embark on your internal marketing journey, I invite you to share your experience (e.g., what works for you, as well as what doesn't) on my internal marketing blog: **www.qualityservicemarketing.blogs.com**. For additional inspiration and ideas, visit my blog routinely, to learn what others are doing.

110

I wish you all the best with your internal marketing!

WORKSHEET #1 – Summarize Your Action Plan Starter Notes

To complete this worksheet, go back and review the results of your mini-audit from Chapter 1 and your Action Plan Starter Notes in Chapters 2, 3, 4, and 6. Then describe what aspects of internal marketing are currently working and what needs to be done in your organization, as outlined below.

Where applicable, note how you intend to implement internal marketing — on a macro (organization-wide) or micro level (specify which departments, divisions, business units, etc.).

Gaining Employee Commitment (Chapter 2): Respecting staff	
What's working that we can continue to do ?	What needs to be done or addressed?

Recognizing staff

What's working that we can continue to do?	What needs to be done or addressed?

Creating/reinforcing a customer-focused culture

What's working that we can continue to do?	What needs to be done or addressed?

Strengthening the Employee-Customer Link (Chapter 3):

What's working that we can continue to do ?	What needs to be done or addressed?

Strengthening the Internal Service Culture (Chapter 4):

What's working that we can continue to do?	What needs to be done or addressed?

Additional notes and comments based on your organization's
current climate:

WORKSHEET #2 – Checklist to Develop Your Internal Marketing Action Plan

Now that you have reviewed the foundation and strategic tools of internal marketing and have identified what is currently working, along with any new or changed initiatives you need to undertake, you are ready to complete the recommended checklist for results described earlier in this chapter.

This worksheet outlines the basic steps you need to develop your customized internal marketing action plan. Based on the summary of your Action Plan Starter Notes from Worksheet #1, complete the steps outlined below to develop your internal marketing action plan. Please note that this is a progressive effort — each successive step is dependent upon completion of the previous step.

Preliminary Step:

Determine who in the organization will be involved in your internal marketing planning and list them here.

I. **Use and or/conduct research to determine how much of an internal marketing effort is needed to instill and/or reinforce customer-focused values.**

    A. First identify and review any sources of in-house customer and employee satisfaction reasearch available.

    B. Use the results found in A to determine what, if any, additional customer and employee research you may need.

117

II. **Segment employees so you can tailor your internal marketing efforts to specific employee groups.** Use whatever segmentation is most appropriate for your organization and internal marketing situation — for instance, length of employment, level of customer-contact, or job function.

    A. Identify which employee segments you intend to target with internal marketing.

III. Set your internal marketing objectives based on your research and what you need to achieve. For example, objectives may include: improve new staff orientation, expand staff training in key areas, create or enhance internal recognition, improve internal communications, increase or maintain levels of employee and/or customer satisfaction.

A. Develop a "wish list" of objectives you would like to accomplish with internal marketing.

B. Prioritize and select the top two or three objectives most critical to your organization.

119

IV. Develop your resulting plan to achieve your selected objectives. Your internal marketing plan may include emphasis on internal media and public relations (e.g., promote success stories, recognize brand ambassadors or marketing heroes); special events (e.g., staff appreciation dinner, customer-focused staff retreats); and any other effort(s) that will strengthen your organization's internal service culture and employee-customer relationships.

   A. List specific internal marketing activities that will help you achieve your objectives. As with any good plan, you will need to be specific regarding the scope of activity, timing, resources, staff responsible, and evaluation.

120

B. Consider how you will manage your internal marketing plan:

    1. How will you get management buy-in for your efforts (overall as well as by specific activity)?

    2. How will you introduce and communicate your internal marketing objectives and supporting activities?

    3. How/when will these activities occur? And in what duration? (For example, a special employee appreciation event may be held on an annual basis, whereas new staff orientation may be held quarterly or more frequently, as needed.)

V. Measure and fine-tune so you can evaluate your efforts relative to your objectives and adapt them as needed.

A. Identify how and when you will measure your results (qualitatively and/or quantitatively).

B. Identify how you will monitor and update your internal marketing efforts.

C. Last, but not least, consider how
you will celebrate your success.

Where It All Started

Very early in my career, I noticed that when employees were considered an after-thought in the marketing of new products and services, there was potential for failure. Forgetting to include employees upfront in the marketing development and launch process sent a clear message — that employee input was unimportant. That left the company with the sudden realization: "Hey, we're getting ready to go to the market next week, and the ad campaign is finalized; shouldn't someone tell the employees about this?"

As a new bank marketer, I thought about all the effort put into developing the campaign, including the two-page spread in Sunday's paper announcing the special sales promotion starting at the bank the next day. What a waste it would be, I found myself thinking, if a customer walked up to a teller's window on Monday morning to ask about the promotion, and the teller said, "I don't know. Nobody told us anything about it."

Obviously, that is no way to make a good impression on customers. And I could only imagine how frustrated the tellers would feel, being put in that position. How could we expect the tellers to effectively serve customers, I wondered, when we weren't doing the same for them? Call it a lack of consideration or respect ... whatever you label it, I was determined not to put my bank's staff in that situation.

That's when I became an advocate for an employees-first approach in my marketing efforts, and thus began my interest-turned-professional passion for internal marketing.

Where It Goes from Here

While the workplace has changed substantially in the 30+ years I've been in it, the need for internal marketing is growing. We live in a fast-paced, global economy where we're connected to work and each other 24/7. My experience has shown, however, that the process of continually communicating with, educating, and motivating employees through internal marketing isn't perceived as very exciting in today's high tech world. Yet, it's precisely because our world is "high tech" that we still need to maintain a level of "high touch."

Internal marketing allows us to apply a high-touch approach to connect employees on three critical levels: to the organization in which they work, to other employees within the organization, and to customers. Internal marketing makes an emotional connection by communicating and reinforcing a sense of common purpose, a sense of belonging, and a sense of being part of something special. This special connection can go a long way in creating the right culture, the right environment, and the right approach for your employees to really embrace the corporate mission and vision to make your organization the success you wish it to be.

Our need for these critical connections is ongoing in these "high tech" times. Technology allows us to reach more people across time and distance in ways never even imagined before, but it can also be insular. Through internal marketing, we can apply the necessary "high touch" approach needed to continue to take care of the people who matter most: our employees and our customers.

Closing Thoughts

Despite my life-long professional passion for internal marketing, as I've matured over the course of my business career, I'm no longer naïve enough to believe that everyone will embrace internal marketing as the best way to serve employees and customers.

Experience has taught me that the organizations who need internal marketing the most (those who give lip service to employee-customer care) are not the ones who will hire me. I've been most successful with the organizations who truly buy into the concept of internal marketing — they're already doing the right things, and they want to do them even better. It's a win-win situation for all: my clients, their employees, their customers, their stakeholders, and me (because I can help make a difference).

Besides helping my clients and colleagues, I knew it was time for me to share internal marketing with others, so they, too, can make a difference in the workplace. I wrote *Taking Care of the People Who Matter Most: A Guide to Employee-Customer Care* to share what I've learned about internal marketing with readers, like you, who want their organizations to do even better.

I'll close now with one of my favorite quotes from Peter F. Drucker, a well known and respected authority on management, about his approach to consulting:

"I feel very strongly that a client who leaves this room feeling he has learned a lot that he didn't know before is a stupid client; either that, or I've done a poor job. He should leave this office saying, 'I know all that — but why haven't I done anything about it?'"[1]

You know what to do with internal marketing. I hope you enjoy doing it.

Notes

Foreword

1) John A. Byrne, "How to Lead Now: Getting Extraordinary PerformanceWhen You can't Pay for It, Fast Company, August 2003, 64.

2) Allen Paison, (partner, Loyalty Research Center, http://www. loyaltyresearch.com), in telephone interview with the author, January 23, 2007.

3) Maritz Research, Maritz Poll Findings, "How to Manage Employees in an Era of Mistrust – Caring is Key to Workplace Harmony," http:// www.maritzresearch.com/release.asp?rc=294&p=1&T=P (accessed October 11, 2006).

Chapter 1

1) Frances Hesselbein, *Hesselbein on Leadership* (San Francisco: Jossey-Bass, 2002), 33.

2) Frederick F. Reichheld, "Lead for Loyalty," *Harvard Business Review*, July–August 2001, 78.

3) D. Randall Brandt and Rodger Stotz, "Grow Your Business Through Superior Customer Experiences," *The Research Report* 4, vol. 18 (October 2005), http://research.report.oct05.mr-2.us/ feature6.phtml (accessed February 14, 2007).

4) Maritz Customer Experience Subject Matter Experts, Customer Experience Series White Paper, "Delight or Defection: The Pivotal Role of People Inside the Customer Experience," November 2006, http://www.maritz.com/CustomerExperience/default.html (accessed February 13, 2007).

5) Rajendra S. Sisodia, David B. Wolfe and Jagdish N. Sheth, *Firms of Endearment: How World-Class Companies Profit from Passion and Purpose* (Philadelphia: Wharton School Publishing, 2007), 89

6) Thomas L. Legare, "Acting on Customer Feedback," *Marketing Research*, Spring 1996, 47.

129

7)   Michael Fielding, "800-lb. Guerrilla," *Marketing News*, April 15,
     2006, 15 (quoting Levinson in an article).

8)   Leonard L. Berry and A. Parasuraman, *Marketing Services:
     Competing Through Quality* (New York: The Free Press, 1991),
     129.

9)   J.W. Marriott, Jr., and Kathi Ann Brown, *The Spirit to Serve:
     Marriott's Way* (New York: HarperCollins, 1997), 34.

10) Forum for People Performance Management and Measurement,
     Executive Summary of Research Study, "Linking Organizational
     Characteristics to Employee Attitudes and Behavior – A Look
     at the Downstream Effects on Market Response and Financial
     Performance," http://www.performanceforum.org/Linking_
     Organizational_Characteristics_to_Employee_Attitudes_and_
     Behavior.59.0.html (accessed August 14, 2006).

11) Jeffrey W. Jones, Ph.D., "In Search of Excellent Customer
     Service," *Bank Management*, February 1991, 40-41.

12) James L. Heskett, W. Earl Sasser, Jr. and Leonard A. Scheslinger,
     The Service Profit Chain (New York: The Free Press, 1997), 30-33.

13) Maritz Customer Experience White Paper, op. cit.

14) John A. Larson and W. Earl Sasser, "Building Trust through
     Committed Employees," *Marketing Management*, Fall 2000, 44.

15) Nancy S. Alrichs, *Competing for Talent: Key Recruitment and
     Retention Strategies for Becoming an Employer of Choice* (Palo
     Alto: Davies-Black Publishing, 2000), 127.

16) John A. Larson and W. Earl Sasser, op.cit. 44.

17) Nancy S. Alrichs, op.cit.127.

18) Ibid., 8.

19) Valarie A. Zeithaml, Mary Jo Bitner and Dwayne D. Gremler,
     Services Marketing: Integrating Customer Focus Across the Firm,
     4th ed. (New York: McGraw-Hill, 2005), 22-23.

20) Forum for People Performance Management and Measurement,
     Research Study, "Internal Marketing Best Practice Study," 3,
     www.performanceforum.org/Internal_Marketing_Best_Practice_
     Study.63.0.html (accessed August 29, 2006).

21) Jeffrey Pfeffer, "The Real Keys to High Performance," *Leader to Leader,* 8 (Spring 1998), 23-29.

22) Christian Grönroos, *Service Management and Marketing: A Customer Relationship Management Approach, 2nd ed.* (Chichester: John Wiley and Sons, Ltd, 2000), 332-335.

23) Scott Adams, *The Dilbert Principle* (New York: Harper Business, 1996), 63.

Chapter 2

1) Ben Machtiger, "Beware Pitfalls that Kill Branding Efforts," *Marketing News*, March 1, 2004, 21.

2) Lawrence A. Crosby and Sheree L. Johnson, "Watch What I Do," *Marketing Management*, November/December 2003, 10.

3) Nancy S. Alrichs, op. cit., Ch. 1, n. 16, 176.

4) "Management Failing to Connect with Employees at Almost Half of Companies," October 11, 2005 press release found on IABC website www.iabc.com.

5) William Ruch, *Corporate Communication: A Comparison of Japanese and American Practices* (Westport: Quorum Books, 1984) 109. Argyris is known for his work with learning organizations.

6) Carol Sturman, "Dare to Dream," *Leader to Leader*, 23 (Winter 2002) 35-39.

7) John A. Byrne, "How to Lead Now: Getting Extraordinary Performance When You Can't Pay for It," *Fast Company*, August 2003, 65.

8) James L. Heskett, et al., op. cit., Ch. 1, n. 16, 114.

9) Bob Nelson, "Top 10 Ironies of Employee Motivation Programs," *Employee Benefit News*, Sept. 15, 1998, Vol. 13, No. 11, 45.

10) Ibid.

11) Cheryl Dahle, "What Are You Complaining About?" ("Say It Again with Feeling" sidebar), *Fast Company*, May 2001, 68.

12) John Putzier, *Get Weird! 101 Innovative Ways to Make Your Company a Great Place to Work* (NY: AMACOM, 2001) 130.

13) Jon R. Katzenbach, *Why Pride Matters More than Money* (New York: Crown Business, 2003)147-149.

14) Rajendra S. Sisodia,et al., op. cit.., Ch.1, n. 6, 45.

15) Marcus Buckingham and Curt Coffman, *First, Break All the Rules* (New York: Simon and Schuster, 1999) 28.

16) Ibid., 32-34.

17) Sari Kalin, "Nice Guys Finish First," *Darwin Magazine*, October/ November 2000, 87.

18) Vicki J. Powers, "Can You Read My Mind," *Continuous Journey*, June/July 1994.

Chapter 3

1) Leonard L. Berry and A. Parasuraman, op. cit., Ch. 1, n. 6, 129.

2) "Satisfaction Action," *Marketing News*, October 28, 1991.

3) Greg Burris, "Turning Staff into Ambassadors," *NACUBO Business Officer*, December 2003, 22-29.

4) Ibid.

5) Charles Tombazian, Bill Heitzman, Stephen Brown, PhD., and Geoff Zwemke, *Pursuit of the Summit* (Scottsdale, AZ: PowerNotes, 1999), 61.

6) William Band and John Guaspari, "Creating the Customer-Engaged Organization," *Marketing Management*, July/August 2003, 36-37.

7) Susan Greco, "Inside-Out Marketing" ("Spring Training" sidebar), *Inc.*, January 1998, 52. Note: in an e-mail correspondence on January 24, 2007, Claire Ho, Marketing Communications Manager at Quad/Graphics, confirmed this practice continues.

8) Daintry Duffy, "Drive Customer Loyalty," *CIO-100*, August 15, 1999, 78.

9) Christopher Caggiano, "Hands-On CEO's Notebook, *How Do I Improve Customer Service*," Inc., August 1997, 92.

10) Tim Triplett, "When Tracy Speaks, Celestial Listens," *Marketing News*, Oct. 24, 1994, 14. In an e-mail message to the author, March 1, 2007, Shelly L. Ruspakka, Marketing Assistant, New Products and Public Relations, Celestial Seasonings, confirmed this practice continues.

11) "Hands-On Sales and Marketing, Customer Service: Grassroots Problem Solving," *Inc.*, March 1996, 92.

12) "Pat Long, "Customer Loyalty, One Customer at a Time," *Marketing News*, Feb. 3, 1997, 8.

13) Joanne Cleaver, "An Inside Job," *Marketing News*, February 16, 1998: 14.

Chapter 4

1) William J. McEwen, "Marketers: Don't Ignore Your Company's Employees," *Gallup Management Journal*, January 12, 2006.

2) Jerry Want, "When Worlds Collide: Culture Clash," *Journal of Business Strategy*, Vol. 24, No. 4, 2003, 16.

3) Ibid., 19.

4) David Lei and Charles R. Greer, " The Empathetis Organization," *Organizational Dynamics*, Vol. 32, No. 2, 2003, 153.

5) Ibid

6) Valarie Willis, "The Two Faces of Accountability," *The Point, Bluepoint Leadership Development*, www.bluepointleadership.com, Sept. 5, 2006.

7) William J. McEwen, op. cit.

8) Leonard L. Berry, *On Great Service* (New York: The Free Press, 1995), 73-74.

9) Charles Tombazian, Bill Heitzman, Stephen Brown and Geoff Zwemke, *Pursuit of the Summit* (Scottsdale, AZ: PowerNotes, 1999), 66.

10) Suein L. Hwang, "Worker Slogans Find New Home This Side of the Great Wall," *The Wall St. Journal,* Oct. 16, 2002.

11) Stephanie Gruner, "Lasting Impressions," *Inc.*, July 1998, 126.

12) Frances Hesselbein, Marshall Goldsmith and Richard Beckhard, editors, *The Organization of the Future*, (San Francisco: Jossey-Bass), 205.

13) Nancy S. Alrichs, op. cit., Ch. 1, n. 16, 154-155.

14) "Executive Edge" ("In the Know" sidebar), *Continental*, May 2000, 21-22.

15) Jill Rosenfeld, "Down-Home Food, Cutting-Edge Business," *Fast Company*, April 2000, 56-58.

16) "Giving Executives a Field Day," *Working Woman*, March 1992.

17) Lawrence A. Crosby and Sheree L. Johnson, "Watch What I Do," *Marketing Management*, November/December 2003, 10-11.

18) James L. Heskett,et.al., op. cit., Ch. 1, n. 12, 241-242.

19) Lawrence A. Crosby and Sheree L. Johnson, op. cit., 10.

20) J. W. Marriott, Jr., and Kathi Ann Brown, *The Spirit to Serve*, (New York: Harper Business, 1997), 129.

21) Ibid, 127.

22) "Achieving Results through Collaboration," A Forum Special Issues Report (Boston: The Forum Corporation, 1992), 5.

23) Cathy Olofson, "Can We Talk," *Fast Company*, October 1999.

24) Paul Roberts, "Live! From Your Office," *Fast Company*, October 1999.

25) Valorie A. McClelland and Richard E. Wilmot, "Communication: Improve Lateral Communication," *Personnel Journal*, August 1990, 32.

26) Associated Press, "NASA Returning to Mars with Odyssey, Cross Fingers," *Scranton Tribune*, April 3, 2001.

Chapter 5

1) Rajendra S. Sisodia, et al., op. cit., Ch. 1, n. 6, 70.

2) Interview with Robert C. Wood, Chairman; Damon Liever, Senior Vice President, Marketing; and Michael J. Bartoszek, Manager of

Training and Development, July 24, 2000. Information also based on subsequent meetings with Michael Bartoszek, 2000-2003.

3) Forum for People Performance Management and Measurement. "The Six Characteristics of Highly Effective Internal Marketing Programs," www.performanceforum.org/Internal_Marketing_Best_Practice_Study.63.0.html (accessed August 29, 2006).

Chapter 6

1) Hal G. Rosenbluth and Diane McFerrin Peters, *The Customer Comes Second* (New York: HarperBusiness, 2002), 221

2) Anne Fisher, "A Happy Staff Equals Happy Customers," Fortune, July 12, 2004, p. 52.

3) Carol Sturman, "Dare to Dream," *Leader to Leader,* 23 (Winter 2002): 35-39.

4) Anne Fisher, op. cit.

5) Rosenbluth and Peters, op. cit.

6) Douglas R. Pruden and Terry G. Vavra, "Controlling the Grapevine," *Marketing Management*, July/August 2004, 26.

7) Ibid., 27.

8) Alan M. Weber, "Danger: Toxic Company," *Fast Company,* November, 1998, 158.

9) Ibid, 160.

Chapter 7

1) William C. Taylor, "At VeriFone It's a Dog's Life (And They Love It!)" *Fast Company,* Issue 01, October 1995, 115.

2) Richard Spitzer and Michael Swidler, "Using a Marketing Approach to Improve Internal Communications," *Employment Relations Today,* Vol. 30, No. 1, Spring 2003, 72.

3) Charles Tombazian, et al., op. cit., Ch. 4, n. 9, 72.

4)   S. Douglas Pugh, Joerg Dietz, Jack W. Wiley, and Scott M. Brooks,
      "Driving Service Effectiveness through Employee-Customer
      Linkages," *Academy of Management Executive,* Vol. 16, #4, Nov.
      2002, 73-82.

5)   Spitzer and Swidler, op. cit. 74-75.

AFTERWORD

1)   John J. Tarrant, *Drucker: The Man Who Invented the Corporate
      Society* (Boston, Massachusetts: Cahners Books, Inc., 1976) 122.

Recommended Reading and Resources

Firms of Endearment: How World-Class Companies Profit from Passion and Purpose by Rajendra S. Sisodia, David B. Wolfe and Jagdish N. Sheth, Wharton School Publishing, Pearson Education, 2007.

> How successful companies focus on all their stakeholders – including employees and customers – not just shareholders. Destined to become a business classic, this book is about leadership and culture at its best.

Married to the Brand – Why Consumers Bond with Some Brands for Life by William J. McEwen, Gallup Press, 2005.

> Examines the emotional connections consumers have with brands, including employee impact on customer relationships that lead to brand engagement (or disengagement).

Light Their Fire: Using Internal Marketing to Ignite Employee Performance and Wow Your Customers by Susan M. Drake, Michelle J. Gulman and Sara M. Roberts, Dearborn Trade Publishing, 2005.

> Describes how to apply internal marketing/branding to motivate employees with emphasis on employee communications and training.

The Customer Comes Second – Put Your People First and Watch 'Em Kick Butt by Hal F. Rosenbluth and Diane McFerrin Peters, HarperBusiness, 2002.

> In-depth look at how Rosenbluth International built a culture focused on employee care.

Love 'Em or Lose 'Em: Getting Good People to Stay (2nd edition) by Beverly Kaye and Sharon Jordan-Evans, Berrett-Koehler, 2002.

> Lots of great management ideas to engage and retain employees.

Internal Marketing: Tools and Concepts for Customer-Focused Management by Pervaiz K. Ahmed and Mohammed Rafiq, Butterworth-Heinemann, published in association with the Chartered Institute of Marketing, 2002.

> Describes internal marketing theory and best practices with applications to total quality management, new product development, and knowledge management.

Linking Customer and Employee Satisfaction to the Bottom Line: A Comprehensive Guide to Establishing the Impact of Customer and Employee Satisfaction on Critical Business Outcomes by Derek Allen and Morris Wilburn, ASQ Quality Press, 2002.

> Statistical and analytic techniques to measure employee-customer linkages.

Get Weird! 101 Innovative Ways to Make Your Company a Great Place to Work by John Putzier, AMACOM, 2001.

> Lots of great ideas to enhance staff recruitment, retention, and recognition.

Fish! A Remarkable Way to Boost Morale and Improve Results by Stephen C. Lundin, Ph.D., Harry Paul and John Christensen, Hyperion, 2000.

> Fast, easy read for a unique approach to re-energizing one's workplace.

Competing for Talent: Key Recruitment and Retention Strategies for Becoming an Employer of Choice by Nancy S. Alrichs, Davies-Black Publishing, 2000.

> Focuses on recruitment and retention strategies from a human resources perspective; explains how to calculate the true cost of employee turnover.

Pursuit of the Summit (Attracting and Retaining the Best Employees and Customers) by Charles Tombazian; Bill Heitzman; Stephen P. Brown, PhD; and Geoff Zwemke, PowerNotes, 1999.

> Summary notes, quotes, and applicable ideas from Arizona State University's Center for Services Leadership outstanding annual symposium. This and other symposium summaries are available at **www.avnet.com/services.**

Discovering the Soul of Service by Leonard L. Berry, The Free Press, 1999.

> Great examples of successful service cultures and values-driven leadership.

The Service Profit Chain: How Leading Companies Link Profit and Growth to Loyalty, Satisfaction, and Value, by James L. Heskett, W. Earl Sasser, Jr., and Leonard A. Schlesinger, The Free Press, 1997.

> Management classic.

Web Resources:

www.performanceforum.org – check out the Forum for People Performance Management and Measurement and its research on Internal Marketing Best Practices.

www.qualityservicemarketing.blogs.com – Quality Service Marketing's blog focused on internal marketing and communications.

143

About the Author

Sybil F. Stershic is a marketing and organizational advisor with more than 30 years of experience helping service providers strengthen relationships with customers and employees. She specializes in internal marketing and marketing/strategic planning facilitation. In addition, she teaches marketing workshops nationwide for corporate and nonprofit professionals.

A graduate of Lehigh University, Sybil began her career in bank marketing. (She worked for several banks that were eventually merged into oblivion.) She founded Quality Service Marketing in 1988 to further pursue her interest in internal marketing. Active in leadership and professional development, Sybil is a former chairman of the American Marketing Association. She lives with her family in the Lehigh Valley, PA region.

Gift?

Reading group?

Training material?

Order more copies of
*Taking Care of the
People Who Matter Most*
online at: